WONDER

AND

WORSHIP

NEW YORK/PARAMUS/TORONT

WONDER AND WORSHIP

JAMES CARROLL

PAULIST PRESS

Designed and Illustrated by Emil Antonucci
Cover photo by Fortune Monte

Copyright © 1970 by
The Missionary Society of
St. Paul the Apostle
in the State of New York

Library of Congress
Catalog Card Number: 70-133469

ISBN: 0-8091-1871-8

Published by Paulist Press
Editorial Office: 1865 Broadway, N.Y., N.Y.   10023
Business Office: Paramus, New Jersey   07652

Printed and bound in the
United States of America

For Joe,
Brian, Dennis,
Kevin
who shared the gift of childhood
with me.

CONTENTS

FAIRY TALES

FOREWORD

Central to the contemporary experience of
man, with special significance for the religious
dimensions of that experience, is his
increasing sensitivity to the adventure and the
excitement that rightfully belong to the
process of human history. "Earth Day," as a
rite of spring in the first year of the 1970's,
might have seemed like an improbable or
frivolous phenomenon to the man of
1960. But for us it was serious and wonderful.
It signified not only the disaster of reckless
pollution as an evil, but also pointed to a
genuine reverence for the richness of our
earthly experience. In fact, earth and
the things of earth have more and more
become for us a reason to celebrate, because
we sense, understand, imagine, and
experience them as good. Moreover, man's
life, world, and history appear all the
more exciting in the vision that we have of
them as taking place in the creative presence
of God. The mystery of man is, quite literally,
immeasurably enhanced by the mystery
of God.

Liturgical renewal has been a leading
question of our day. It is, in reality, a way of
asking how we may remind and help each
other, when we come together to pray, to
experience and surrender to the mystery of

God's presence and to the signs that he makes of himself and his presence in our history. Sam Keen writes in his delightful book **To a Dancing God** that one of the ways traditional man sought to achieve and preserve a sense of personal identity was "to tell a story that placed his life within an ultimate context." Of course. And the story of God's relationship with man, as told in scripture, describes the sacred and radical context of human experience in such moving terms that, for thousands of years, the scriptural account of this story has held an honored place in the forms and shape of Jewish and Christian worship services.

The present volume represents an attempt to stir that same sense of wonder and celebration by telling the story in different ways. Like classical liturgical **anamnesis,** the preoccupation of these tales and stories is not so much with past events as such, but rather with the experienced awareness and acknowledgment of God's eternal reality, and wonder over the ways in which he has revealed himself within the dimensions of man's time and history and, hopefully, will continue to do. The traditional "memorial," as any reading of the texts makes clear, is no exercise in psychological recall, but is, rather, concerned with past, present and what will be, in fulfillment of the promise.

We have, perhaps, too often thought that reforming the liturgy meant simply reforming liturgical texts: More recently it has become clear that concern should be shown more for the experience than for the text (or rubric). Often enough our excessively cerebral interest in textual formularies has drawn our attention away from the very realities proclaimed by the text. For all of these reasons, Father Carroll's imaginative retelling of the story of salvation and life carries with it the hopeful possibility of turning us toward mystery and the unsuspected reality of God.

John Gallen, S.J.
Woodstock Center for Religion and Worship

Introduction

Our world will not be wonderful until we ourselves are full of wonder. We have this cherished need for the world and ourselves and each other to be wonderful. We have this cherished need to push beyond the limits of the ordinary, to discover what belief and hope claim is there—a mystery place of awe and true communion. Solitude and silence, prayer and liturgy, symbol and sharing—these are the ways we have of waiting for wonder to come again.

This collection of tales comes out of my own waiting for wonder. They are born of a world beyond dailiness, and they enshrine the gifts of awe and true communion for which we yearn. I offer them to you in the hope that your waiting for wonder will be helped, quickened, whether in silence or song, whether in solitude or in the common sharing of worship.

Fairy tales are among the most useful and, at once, the most maligned of the imaginative genres. Most useful because they hit **mystery** head on, releasing the wild and creative resources of human fantasy. Harvey Cox writes: "Fantasy is the richest source of human creativity. Theologically speaking, it is the image of the creator God in man." If we allow ourselves to enter into the fantasy world of tales, we will discover there the main notes of prayer: mystery, awe, hope, silence, the word, solitude, and communion.

But it is difficult for us to do that. Our fantasy lives are suspect even to ourselves, and dreams embarrass us. As for fairy tales, we have long since left them to the children. And children know what a mistake we have made. Perhaps they don't tell us because our adult indifference makes the world of fairy tales all the more theirs.

A fairy tale is the imagination made available in a unique and powerful way. Fairy tales are not mere allegories or stories with moral lessons. What is important about a tale is the experience of exploring a strange land that may, after all, be home. More precious than any allegory, a fairy tale invites us into the fantastic world of awesome fear, trembling, wonder, fascination, joy, play, dread, and love.

Fairy tales fully seduce wonder out of us, and they do so in a manner that suits the strange and ambiguous thing it is to be a human being. Thus, a fairy tale is a matter mainly of tone, atmosphere, and feeling. It is concerned less with plot or character than with the faint tissue of living. As Tolkien says, "**Faerie** cannot be caught in a net of words, for it is one of its qualities to be indescribable, though not imperceptible."

One of the prejudices of our culture is

that the world of fantasy and tale is an "unreal" world which stands in opposition to the "real" world of our daily existence. This is not so. The world of fantasy is not less real than the world of fact. In some ways it is more real. The world opened to us by fairy tales is indeed our own daily world, good and bad, fun and hard, but it is experienced in depth, in mystery, in wonder. Fairy tales invite us to live more deeply in this very world we call "real."

Out of my own experience of its fruitfulness, I propose a marriage between the life of fantasy and the life of faith, between fairy tales and worship, whether in solitude or in liturgy. I have no impulse simply to make worship a "meaningful experience" by bringing together two ordinarily unrelated worlds. On the contrary, I propose the marriage because fairy tales and worship derive from precisely the same source in man. They already share a commonness we do not usually see. When Harvey Cox writes that religious ritual is "embodied fantasy," he is telling us that the impulse to fantasize underlies the impulse to worship. When Tolkien writes that fairy tales "seek to satisfy the primordial desire of man to hold communion with all that is," he is telling us that the mystical yearnings of men are at the heart of fairy tales.

The very desires that well up in us as prayer and the very fullness that wells up in us as praise give rise to fairy tales. The craving for union with all things in their extra-human source issues both in religious ritual and in tales. And so it is that the tales gathered here claim as home the world of wonder and the world of worship. And they proclaim that these two worlds are one.

Suggestions for Use

These tales can be used in a variety of settings as invitations to the human experiences of wonder and worship.

In Solitude. Break your routine. Go to a place where you can be creatively alone. If the weather is good, go outside. If you live near a forest or a park, go there. Declare the silence. The tales are short; read each one through as a piece. Be alert to the hopes and fears it touches in you. Allow them to grow into tales of your own. Allow your fantasy to wander into whatever prayer is for you.

In the Family. Parents and children alike can share these tales. Gather the family and take turns reading the tales aloud. Don't be afraid to dramatize. Encourage the children to retell the story. See if you can make up tales of your own. Someone can begin and close the gathering with a spontaneous prayer, such as: "God, help us to live happily ever after with each other and you."

In Groups. Prayer groups and discussion groups can find the tales useful for the **experience** of wonder they offer. Resist the urge to allegorize or draw moral lessons. The object is the experience of the fantasy world, not sermonizing. Groups may want to respond to the tales by creating their own group fantasies, by acting out the tales, or by praying out of the shared wonder.

In Eucharistic Settings. These tales are appropriate for use in the context of the Eucharist. Most of the tales should be read aloud by one person, though several are suited for telling by several persons, each taking the part of a different character. The story teller may want to relate the tale in his own words.

If children are present, gather them around the story teller, sitting on the floor if possible. Informality helps. Several kinds of common responses are possible after the tale is told. The children present can be asked to share their feelings about the tale. Children take more freely to fantasy than most of us. Their responses can be remarkable and facilitating.

If the community is not too large, they may want to create their own tales out of the issues of their own lives. If the group seems too large, break it down into smaller ones.

Non-verbal responses may be appropriate, whether some kind of informal dramatic recreation or drawing pictures that try to catch the mood.

Sometimes the fullness of silence is the best response. Perhaps a break before the bread and wine would be appropriate. People could seek out silence, go for a walk with their own imaginings, or share informally with others.

The Eucharistic Prayer included in this book can be used as a proclamation of the good news that, in Jesus, the timelessness of fantasy is joined to history, for the moment of our salvation is not "once upon a time" but "the night before he died."

Resonating Scripture Themes. Included here are references to passages from the scriptures that strike sympathetic chords with the tales in this book. They do not intend to explain or illustrate one another, but only to invite the discovery that the Word of God springs from the timeless wonders of man.

Calls to Worship. Also included are three sample calls to worship which may be used to introduce a worship experience built around the tales. You may want to compose introductions that lift up the specific themes being treated.

Calls To Worship

I Fairy tales are for children, for the children
who live, alive, in each of us, yet waiting to
laugh again and be set free to play. They wait
to laugh and play not because they are
irresponsible or because they haven't heard
the worldwide bad news of now, but because
they have heard the good news of
Jesus Christ.

The good news we gather to celebrate is
that the timeless yearnings of men have taken
flesh in a man. Now there is nothing that
does not speak to us of God, if only we know
how to hear. Now even the hidden hopes
and fears that spin out nets of Story can
speak to us of great care. It is the great care
of God and his fantastic Son for us. Let us
listen and hear.

II We live in the shadow of catastrophe, yet
we gather here in hope and joy. There are
dreamers among us, men of vision and
far-reaching fantasy. They are waiting to be
heard.

Their news from the realm of tales is simple,
straightforward, and good. Their news is that
the final catastrophe for men, the final
unexpected, sudden turn of time has already
occurred. It was a sudden turn of grace.
It was a catastrophe of goodness, for the
Word of God was flesh for us and his name

22

was Jesus. The dreamers among us are
ourselves and our news in his name is that
now the happy ending is no more child's wish,
but the way it will be for us and for all
creation. Let us listen and hear.

III We are wishers, waiters-out of wonder
and hope. We gather in song and silence to
hear in new ways the Word of the vision and
the dream and, indeed, the fantasy that
has sent shivers of excitement through the
flesh of a billion human beings.

We gather to proclaim to each other and to
hear again the good news that our hiddenmost
fantasy is history now. Jesus died and lives
still. He unhides himself in the strange,
mysterious world from which tales come. They
come to us as hints that the wonder-filled
realm of fantasy for us is nothing less than
the kingdom of God. Let us listen and hear.

FAIRY TALES

PIERCING OF SPIDERLAND

There was once a tiny little man called
Piercing, who lived on the minute-hand of the
big village clock. No one was quite sure how
he came to live there, not even Piercing
himself. As a little boy, before Piercing lived
in the clock, he remembered how everyone
would say there was never enough time, would
say there should be a way of slowing down
the hands of the clock. Piercing never felt
like he needed more time until he got his idea
for the story of spiderland. It would be the
story of the little world of the beautiful,
silver-rope spider webs, the world of the
boulder-drops of rain. But there was too much
to write. Piercing was afraid to begin the story
because there might not be enough time to
finish it. If only there was some way to slow
down time.

That was what Piercing was thinking as he
went to sleep for the last time in a bed. When
he woke up he was sitting on the minute-hand
of the village clock. He soon found that by
crossing his legs he could balance his writing
book well enough to write. And so it was
that, on the hand of the clock, Piercing was
able to slow time down while spinning out the
story of spiderland. There were difficulties, of
course. The twelve and the six were the
biggest problem, and the people of the

village were a problem too. Whenever the minute-hand began to sink past the four or climb by the ten, Piercing had to stop writing and take a firm hold on the slick moving needle. Otherwise he would slide off. This meant that he spent as much time of each hour clinging to the clock as he did writing. He might not have minded this but for the way his neighbors carried on. They laughed. As the minute-hand steepened itself, they would begin to gather in the square of the village in front of the station. They came not to watch the clock, but to watch Piercing. He knew they came to see him fall, but he was always able to hold on. They always laughed and jeered at him as the minute-hand passed four or ten, but when it touched the six or the twelve a strange stillness always fell over the crowd. It was then that Piercing had to clutch the hardest, then that he had to squeeze with all his might to keep from falling. Both moments were bad, but the moment of six was the worst. The hand was straight down. It was an excruciating moment, and it was then that time passed most slowly of all.

Nine and three were splendid. It was at those moments that Piercing did his best writing. It was then that spiderland came most alive. Spiderland was a fine and silver web that always glistened in an early morning dew. There were innumerable jewels of water

swinging in a slight breeze that made a kind of
amber music. Through the perfect ladders of
the web, a country opened out and there were
glimpses of trees marching over hills, and of
mountains kissed by clouds with snow.
There were strange birds that dashed back
and forth carrying messages for the branches
of the trees. The air was pure enough to see,
and it was green and golden. Tying everything
together was the magnificent web that
quivered its way from the smallest drop of
rain through the bloom of every curving twig
to mighty mountains. And such was that web
that there was a vast sweep of grass within
its embrace, and such was that web that every
blade could be seen green and close distinctly.
The trees held the charm of distance, yet
had the feel of being near. Such was that web.
Piercing wrote a world and it was wild with
perfume and peace.

There was one disturbance about spiderland.
As much as Piercing would write and wander
through the green and webbed golden, as
much as he searched it out and scribbled
about, he could not find the spider. It was a
spiderland without the spider. The web was
everything, the glistener, the tier-together, the
astonisher of birds. The spider's web was the
wire on which raindrops danced their
stunning dance, the wire that brought
distances near and made mountains breathless

and available. But the spider was nowhere to
be seen. Piercing, and the world he wrote,
could never rest quite comfortable with
this. He was afraid of the spider because it
was not there.

One day, after a long, long time of sitting on
the minute-hand of the village clock, Piercing
went about as usual writing out the story
of spiderland. The villagers gathered as usual
as the minute-hand sank slowly by the three.
But something was different this day. Piercing
didn't notice the laughing or jeering, for
there was a fever about his writing. There was
a low thunder in spiderland, constant, close
and menacing. Piercing felt a fear welling up
strong inside him. He wrote and wrote. And
there was a fever about spiderland. Something
different was happening and Piercing didn't
know at first what it was. But as he wrote
and wrote he began to see that the glistening
web of all the world's everything was being
spun backward, being sucked away from drops
of rain and the green golden air of astonishing
birds. The web was being woven away,
spooled up quick and ragged by some fury
from the other side of the rumbling mountains.
The thunder grew lower and louder. It was
then that Piercing knew that the spider was
coming to spiderland. And, oh, what a coming
it was! The skies shook and the trees tried to
crawl away. The sweep of grass rolled like

any oceans of typhoon. The worlds of the web were being undone. All was a stare. The birds and Piercing hovered in their fright, but only Piercing, of all the creatures alive, continued to write.

The people in the village square were not laughing. They stood still as any August, staring up at the clock. The minute-hand was slipping toward five and Piercing was yet cross-legged and writing. He had not begun to clutch. They did not see what he saw, but they saw him seeing. Some wanted to shout for him to hold on, but there was no sound. They did not see the mountains moving as Piercing did. The mountains moving away from the distance, running fast as any boy toward the broken center of the web. Piercing heard the birds screaming messages of fear. Spiderland was looking to him for help. But he could only quiver out the words of terror, for the spider was coming after him as well. The violence of the screamings and the fury of the thunder grew and grew. Piercing could not close his eyes, could not run, could not stop the story of spiderland. And so it was that, when the minute-hand was nearly at six that day, in front of all his neighbors, Piercing fell.

Piercing's neighbors tried to find his little body to give him a proper burial. But they were never able to do it: He had fallen from the minute-hand through a large crack in the bottom of the face of the village clock. Several of the more agile men climbed up to get the body out, but they could not get through the crack, for they were of normal size. They reported that there was no sign of Piercing, that nothing of him could be seen in the darkness of the clock. There was only, they said, a large spider that ate small bits of paper and was busy spinning out the most beautiful web they had ever seen.

Theme and Resonating Scripture
Day of the Lord
Revelation 4, 1-8

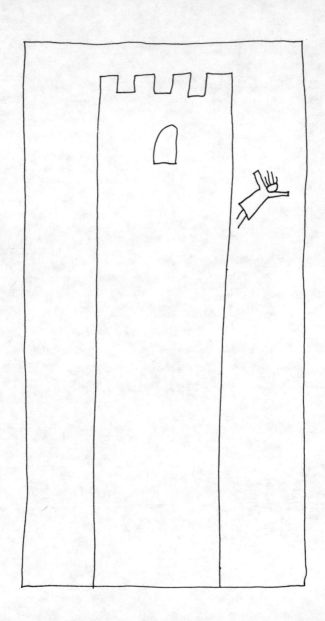

BANISH THE WIZARD

In the time of everywhen, the time of when
wishes, good and bad, came true quite often,
there lived a spinning-woman. She was not
old, though neither was she young. She
worked all day of all her years turning coarse
flax into soft thread, and thread into fine
clothes. She was both spinning-woman and
seamstress for all the villagers, and even for
some of the poorer courtiers who lived in the
castle on the hill. The lord of the realm lived
there too, but his spinning and sewing
were done in a faraway, richer land.

For years and years, ever since memory,
the spinning-woman had had a heavy, heavy
heart. It was, she felt at times, as if her inner
flesh were made of iron, as if all her hidden
aprilness were the dust on one single,
hard-blown leaf of October. She did not know
the why of her silent desperation, but only
the weight of it. It was a weight she was
quite alone with. For, though all the village
folk came to her for their spinning and sewing,
and though her skillful work was loved and
admired, the spinning-woman herself never
was. She was even jealous, at times, of the
clothes she made, for they went off to be
intimate with an owner while she locked up
her shop each night alone. Every now and then
she thought, if only she had this or that, if

only such and such was so, the air would.be, both within her and without, a little lighter, easier to breathe. It so happens that at the moment when this story began the spinning-woman was thinking that she would be happy at last if only she were called upon to spin her thread and make a robe for the king himself. Even her heavy loneliness would not survive such a privileged task of joy.

And so it was, for such were those days, that by a strange and not quite stroke of accident, the spinning-woman was visited by a man who said he was from the castle of the king. She was startled when she opened the door of her shop, for the man who had knocked was the one the villagers called the king's wizard. He was dressed in a black gown that reached to the ground and flashed with rich jewels of many colors. The woman saw that he carried a large and heavy looking bundle in his arms. He stood looking at her with eyes that were deep and dangerous. When at last he entered her shop he told that he had come with a command from the king. She was to take the quantity of gold he gave her—it was the bundle he carried—and she was to spin it into fine gold thread. From the thread she was to weave fine gold cloth, and from the cloth she was to make a fine gold gown to be worn by the king at the great festival. The spinning-woman knew of no festival, and was puzzled further as to why the king should select her for such a task. She spoke none of her questions, for the eyes of the one they called the wizard filled her with fear. He said he would return for the gown before the moon came again, and then he was gone.

The spinning-woman was perplexed. She had little time in which to accomplish the difficult task of such a gold gown, and yet she could not bring herself, try as she would, to begin. She was pleased to have been chosen, yet still she wondered why. There was an edge of terror about the task, perhaps a lingering of the wizard's stare. Thus it was that the heaviness of her heart had not gone away at all, as she had imagined it would.

Outside the window of the spinning-woman's little shop there were birds talking in the trees. The woman was sitting quite still before the quantity of gold, wanting to begin to spin, yet unable to do so. She heard the birds and began to listen closely to them. It may be that what she heard then were not words spoken by the birds at all, but she did hear words, and they seemed wise to her. She heard that the spinning of gold is a task of such infinite delicacy that only a light and free heart can accomplish it. She heard that some are born with such a heart, and that others must seek it out. She heard that there is a potion for the heavy-hearted and that it could be had that very day from a roaming troubador who waited by the well outside the village.

The spinning-woman took a small, but very precious, part of the gold. She thought to herself that she would go to the well and offer that part of gold for the potion that would lighten her heart. She was fearful as she left her shop, for she knew the wizard would be angry if he discovered her theft of gold. She shuddered to think of the king's anger. It would be even worse than the wizard's. She put the thought out of her mind.

Sure enough, when the spinning-woman arrived at the well, a troubador was sitting at its edge. He was ragged and looked poor, which quickened her hope, for surely he would take the gold. She approached him and spoke. "Sir, I know you have a potion of great power. I have the heaviest of hearts, and I would have it to be lightened." The troubador was silent for a moment, and then he said, "I see that your heart is heavy, but what great power do you think I have?" The woman grew more anxious. "You have a potion of the power that will free my heart to do what it must do. I will pay you this precious·gold." The troubador was silent for another moment and then he said, "Your gold is of less value to me than the water of this well."

The woman saw that the eyes of the troubador were even deeper than the wizard's. There was not danger in them, though, but only the strangest kind of blue tenderness. After a moment she said, "You have no magic potion, then?" He replied, "You speak truly. I have no magic. I have only this water." He looked into the well, and continued, "This water can be a potion of forever's delight if it is drunk with me and the company of my followers." The woman asked, "Who are your followers?" The man pointed to a group of men and women who were gathered in a small camp a little way off. They were playing soft string instruments and singing quietly. The troubador and the spinning-woman listened for a time. Then he said, "We have no use for stolen gold. It is the heaviest of all burdens and we travel lightly." The woman knew then that she was herself known. It was his eyes that made her breathing slow. She said, "I was hoping you might help me, for I grow desperate." The troubador said, "We have made a place for you in our caravan. The jar from which we will drink this water is a jar for you, if you wish it." The woman looked at the man, and then at the others in the distance. She saw that they were poorly dressed and that they bore the marks of a hard life. She thought of her little shop, of all the gold, and of the joy that would be hers if only she could begin to weave the gown for the king. She looked at the troubador's eyes, and, though the memory of the wizard's still frightened her, she turned from them and went away. She went away sad.

On the night of the moon's return the spinning-woman still had not begun to spin the gold, for her heart was heavier than ever. She sat alone and afraid, for she knew the king's wizard was coming. She was nevertheless startled at the knock on the door of her shop. When the wizard entered the room he was immediately angry, for the gold was still open on the table, open and unspun. He shouted at her, "Where is the king's gown?" The spinning-woman explained to the wizard that gold is unable to be spun by one of such a heavy heart as hers. She told him of the magic potion that lightens hearts, but which she was unable to obtain. At this the wizard's furor eased a bit, and he fell into deep thought. When he spoke at last, his deep and dangerous eyes flashed. "I have such a potion in my keeping. You shall drink it tonight and such will be the delicacy of your spinning that the gold thread will be doubly fine and you shall make two gold gowns, instead of one." The spinning-woman asked, "For whom will be the second gold gown?" The wizard said, "The gown will be mine, and all its kingly power will be mine as well. You shall never speak of it to anyone."

At this the spinning-woman was more frightened than ever, for this was indeed a theft not merely of gold, but of what was most sacred in all the realm. Still, her hopes for the joy of spinning and weaving the king's gown made it impossible to resist the wizard. She looked into the wizard's deep and dangerous eyes and she nodded her head ever so slightly.

The wizard took the spinning-woman and the gold to the castle. Since it was night and the moon had gone down, no one was able to see them. They crossed the wide moat on a narrow footbridge that creaked out the only noise of their passage. They moved quietly through long dark corridors until finally they came to a tower in the most remote part of the great stone castle on the hill. The wizard led the spinning-woman up a narrow and winding stairway of stone. After they had climbed for some time they came to a large dark room that smelt of mystery and had a chill of fear about it. There the wizard busied himself over several large jars while the woman waited. At last he came to her with a dram of ugly liquid. Without a word she drank.

The spinning-woman was spinning then. She did not know where the wheel of her work had come from, nor did she wonder about it —so furious was she about treading the paddle and pulling the thread through the tugging loop. She worked blindly and with a passion, not seeing either the gold or the thread that she twisted and pulled. What she saw instead was a spinning vision of never-ending roads on which she herself was running. She saw hills, and beyond them hills again, all of which she was climbing, sweating, working to pass over. She saw herself falling and rising to begin again. She saw boulders that waited to be pushed to the peaks of all the hills. And she saw, clearly and up close, a heart. It was bound around with bands of iron and she saw them tighten, squeezing life and blood, pressing hard against the soft and yielding red flesh. She saw the bound and heavy heart and knew from the pain that broke inside her breast that the heart she saw was her own.

Then, out of nowhere, from no expectable, the wizard struck the spinning-woman viciously. He knocked her from the wheel and broke the visions of her treading. There was a fury about him, and the woman saw that the danger of his eyes filled the dark room. He screamed at her. "The thread is not gold! Where is the gold?" She looked at the thread of her work piled high around her. It was, indeed, not gold, but the coarse thread of cloth for making sacks. The wizard stood over her and badgered her with frenzy. "What have you done? Where is the gold?" The spinning-woman was not terrified, but rather numb. The iron of her heart's bondage had cut something like despair into her. Such was that wound that there was nothing left to fear. She could neither rise nor fall again. She waited for the wizard's fury to spend itself on her final death.

It was then, at that very moment, that the sounds of stringed instruments drifted lightly into the tower room. The spinning-woman remembered the sound. She had heard it by the well on the edge of the village. She had heard it with the troubador. It was the playing of his caravan. She saw in the far corner of the room the grey outline of a window. It was at the sound of the music and the memory of the troubador and the sight of the window that the woman's heart leapt. It leapt just enough and with such slight force, but force nonetheless, that the iron bands broke, and she was all at once on her feet, across the room and at the window. And such was that moment that not only her dead heart was enabled to leap with life, but so was she. She leapt from the window of the tower.

The spinning-woman's falling was a strange mixture of not knowing what or why had happened and knowing that the troubador was there after all. Her falling was less heavy than she expected, for her heart was without iron. She fell into the moat of the castle with a splash that was part of the music being played. And then many hands were pulling her and many arms were holding her, and then carrying her, wet and new from the dark water. When her eyes adjusted to the sharp light of sunrise she saw that the troubador himself was holding her. He looked at her with the same deep eyes of before and said, "How light and easy you are!" She saw then that he was dressed in a long gold gown. It was soft against her cheek. She said, "Are you, then, the king?" He said, "Yes." She said, "My lord, you know what wrong I have done. Forgive me." The king said nothing, but all the people gathered round them in a great circle of embrace. The woman asked him, "Why, sir, do you not banish the wizard?" The king looked at all his people and then at her, and said, "I banish him repeatedly, but you my people keep bringing him back." At this the woman thought for a moment, and then she asked one final question: "Why is there a festival, Lord?" He smiled at her and said, "The festival is you." At that the spinning-woman also smiled, and, as it turns out, she was, with that smile, very young and lovely.

Theme and Resonating Scripture
Forgiveness
John 4, 5-26

OLLIE INCOMFRY

Before going up in the blue hills, the fat and
ugly man stopped. He turned to look back at
the city he was leaving. He saw the spires of all
the buildings. He saw the smoke of all the
fires. He stumbled his eyes to the dark river
that cut the heart out of the city. It ran like
black blood through the oldest, dirtiest district.
The district where the house where his room
had been. The lady who lived on the bottom
floor might wonder where he went to, fat and
ugly. She would miss his money maybe. He
always left it in her box. Except this once when
he kept the money there days past time,
hoping she would come up to his room to ask
for it. He thought perhaps they could talk
about something. He had tea on the fire those
three days, waiting. But three long days went
by. She did not come up. So it was that, after
putting the money in a box on the bottom
floor three days late, he decided he would
leave. The fat and ugly man stood looking at
the city before going up into the blue hills. He
remembered the game of years before, how
there was for all the children a sizzling panic
of running, hiding, and crouching very still, the
holding of breath just before being found. He
remembered how after an age of watching
from afar, fat and ugly even then, he finally
joined the game, desperate to be found. He

remembered how he crawled under a straggly bush and held his breath too soon. He was, of all the children, the one least hidden. He was, of all the children, the one least sought. He was never found that day, years before. He held his breath and was never found. And so it was that he stood looking for the last time at the spired hiding place of all his years.

The hills beyond the city were blue. They were blue from a distance, blue if looked at from the second floor window of a house by the black river that cut through the heart of the city. But the hills were blue, as the fat and ugly man saw, if you walked into them too. They were, unlike most hills, blue from up close. There were blue bushes and the tall grass, only tinged with green, was also mainly blue. The trees of the hills were few at first, but they moved closer together the farther up he went. As if for warmth, for it was cool. Even the cool was blue. The fat and ugly man was not afraid, though he had never been in the hills before, though he had never been amid so many trees. He walked slowly looking. There were birds blinking past pieces of sky above him. There were bees hanging around each other in blue bunches, like grapes. There were needles of light that gathered in bits of dust. There were threads of spider webs that sewed leaves together. Shadows hummed with silence. After walking for most of the day, the fat and ugly man stopped to listen. Even the stillness was blue. He sat on soft moss, and then lay back, resting, breathing. The world was new. It was blue. It was soft and easy.

The voices were a surprise, but not as strange or frightening as they might have been at another time or another place. They were young and singing, from another world, it seemed. "Ollie." They sang a name. "Ol-lie." The fat and ugly man lifted his head slightly. The silence floated away under the light weight of young music:

Ollie went to the hills to hide his face, but the hills sing out: "No Hiding Place. There's no Hiding Place up here."

The voices—they were voices of children— were still for a moment. They chanted high and slow again "Ol-lie." They were closer. "Ol-lie, Ol-lie, Ollie, Ollie Incomfreee." The fat and ugly man sat up then, for the voices were very close indeed.

"Hello, Ollie." It was a little girl. The fat and ugly man squeezed and quickly unsqueezed his eyes. "Hello Ollie." There was another little girl, and then—"Hello, Ollie." A little red-headed boy. They were four feet tall or less, and they stood only a breath away, smiling. One of the girls, golden haired, the one who had spoken first, held a rubber ball in her hands. The other girl had hair the color

of deep water on a dark day. She said again
"Hello, Ollie." The fat and ugly man felt a fear
for the first time in the hills. It was fear of
the eyes that were stunning him. The eyes of
the children made him shudder. He closed his
own and covered them. After a moment, the
boy spoke softly and low. "Please, please,
Ollie, open your eyes. Please open your eyes.
Your eyes, Ollie. We need your eyes." The
fat and ugly man only squeezed his eyes
tighter and pressed his hands harder over
them. For this was very strange.

One of the little girls spoke then. "Ollie,
please open your eyes. Please, Ollie, please."
And then the other girl said, "Ollie, these are
the blue hills. Everything that matters here is
blue. Blue is the color of birds, it is the sound
of quiet, it is the feel of morning. Ollie,
everything good is blue but our eyes. My eyes
are brown." Then the other girl said, "My
eyes are green, Ollie." And the boy said, "My
eyes are almost red. What color are your eyes,
Ollie?" The fat and ugly man knew they
were talking to him, though he hadn't any
idea why they called him Ollie, for it wasn't his
name at all. He held his eyes shut hard as
ever, for he was still afraid. He did not know
what color his eyes were, and, wondering, he
was surprised that he had never noticed.
There had never, he thought, been anyone to
tell him.

"Ollie, please, if your eyes are blue, ours will be too." It was the little boy who spoke, and so the fat and ugly man said, without taking his hands from his eyes or opening them: "Little boy, who are you? And why do you call me Ollie?" The boy said, "Those are hard questions. We are children like you; we were once game-watchers too, once the hangers-back who never could play for one reason or another. We were too young, or too sick, or too shy. These are the hills of the left out ones. But all the games here are for everyone. Before I was never **called over,** but now I am, and my name is Red Rover."

Then one of the little girls began to speak: "I was never let into the dancing circle when they went Ring around Rosy. But see, Ollie, now I am Rosy and they ring around me." The other girl said, "Whenever we play with a ball here I have a special job. If the ball goes too high, over a fence or wall or something, I run and get it. Everyone shouts my name. They say "'Annie, Annie over.'" The boy said then, "We know about the game of your name, Ollie. Ollie Incomfry. That's your name in these hills because hiding here is always being found, and you are free to stay and play. You are Ollie for us."

The fat and ugly man could feel the wetness of his hands. From tears perhaps, or nervous sweat. He didn't know which or care. He took

his hands down from his face, though his
eyes he kept firmly shut. There was silence
then for several moments and everyone was
quite still. Soon the fat and ugly man heard the
young voices singing again softly as if from
a distance, though he knew they were
still there.

Ollie, Ol-lie, Ol-lie Incomfreee . . .
Ollie went to the hills to hide his face,
but the hills sang out: "No Hiding Place.
There's no Hiding Place up here."

The fat and ugly man felt small hands in his
own, then. They were tugging at him gently.
One of the little girls in sing-song voice said,
"Let's ring around with Ollie," and, still
tugging, all three of the children sang softly,

Let's ring around with Ollie.
Let's ring around with Ollie . . .

The fat and ugly man felt himself being pulled
to his feet, his eyes still closed. There was a
strength in the hands that held his, that made
him feel little bigger, if at all, than the children.
Then all of them, the two girls and the boy
and the fat and ugly man, were moving in a
circle, slowly at first, then dancing faster to the
music. The children were singing loudly now.

Let's make a circle and go around
and be feet full of fun
because Ollie Incomfry is found.

The fat and ugly man began himself to sing.
He was lighter and quicker of step than ever

before. He felt his face full of smile, and so it was that, when they were all out of breath at last and they all crashed down to the ground, he opened his eyes.

"Oh, Ollie," the golden-haired girl said, staring hard at him. The other two just looked. They were silent, all. The four of them sat, still holding hands. The three staring at the one, and one staring back. The fat and ugly man asked finally, "Are they?" No one spoke. He asked again. "Are they blue?" Still no one spoke. The fat and ugly man looked from child to child. When he looked at the boy he felt the hands they held press harder. He looked at the hands and then looked again, harder. His own hand was no bigger than the little boy's. His eye traced its way up his own arm to the rest of his body. It was small again, small as any child's. He was four feet tall or less, thin and not ugly, for children never are. He looked at the other children again. They were all smiling, and the holding hands grew tighter all around. Ollie asked again, "Are my eyes blue?" "No," Annie said. And then Rosy said, "No matter, Ollie. It gives us someone to look for together." Then Red Rover said, "And that's the best game of all, Ollie Incomfry."

Theme and Resonating Scripture
Day of the Lord
Revelation 14, 1-3a. 4-7

CRACKER JACK;
THE SWEET TASTE OF CHILDHOOD

"Oh, for a bird whistle!" cried the meanly young man. It was while he was longing for peace and the past and full youth again that he remembered the prize of childhood. He remembered the tall, narrow box of coated corn and its real plastic toy for finishing. Delight at the whistle with wings came back to him and it seemed that if only he could win that prize again there would be peace and he would still be young. "Oh for a bird whistle," he cried, for he was very much alone and along in life enough to be terrified of growing old.

It was then a very old and wrinkled shopkeeper who sold him the Cracker Jacks at last—his first Cracker Jacks in twenty years at least. He didn't notice the sidelong look of wondering the shopkeeper gave him, for he thought nothing strange of being full-grown and buying children's food. He thought, in fact, only of the winged whistle.

He thought of one day's boy-running to the top of the highest hill for miles and blowing birds alive with plastic. There were birds everywhere, swooping out of time, darting in wild, sky-wide webs, of which he was weaver with his whistle. From far and better lands they carried on their wings cool and crystal air for him to breathe and blow again. And blow the boy did, and only then was there singing on the hill and in its hollows. Such a singing that the trees wrote a dance upon the wind and the flyers joined arms and did it. And blow the boy did and the singing and dancing became a plain full of people, arms joined, legs lifted, alive. A million different faces, one each from every age and place of time, leapt into life. A chorus of laughter to the winged-whistle of one day's boy on the highest hill for miles.

The meanly young man began to eat them, by the single Cracker Jack at first, then by twos, by threes and more. He stopped squeezing his hand into the thin box, turned the box and began to pour. He filled his cheeks and he worked his teeth into and through the sweet taste of childhood. He ate with a passion to finish, but there was more coated corn than one would think for the size of the box. He stuffed it by the handful now into his mouth, spilling mounds and not caring. There was fury and frenzy to finish, but the box would not be emptied. For minutes, then for hours he ate. He had bought, as it was turning out, a bottomless box of Cracker Jacks.

A number of years later the man was no longer meanly young. He was meanly old. The Cracker Jacks by then were stale but still coming. He had grown to be quite fat. He had difficulty breathing; though he ate slowly without the passion of before, still he fed himself fistful after fistful of coated corn. His arm and his jaws worked continually in the steady rhythm of perfect habit.

The sweet taste of childhood was long since gone, and gone long since was the memory of why and how he began to eat. Eating by then was all there was to do. He had become himself a box of Cracker Jacks with no bottom and no hope for one. Which wasn't all that bad—being dull, it's true, but never hard against the pain of hunger. Since the past and its painful yearning had been swallowed away, and since the future had become an infinity of food, there was about the present a quiet that could have passed for peace. In such a world of no expectation and therefore of no disappointment, in such a world where things could, as they say, be worse, the man grew ever shorter of breath. He grew ever less young until, finally, one day, he was old.

He was old on the day his hand, not expecting to at all, touched the bottom of the box. His breath stopped at once. He couldn't breathe at all. He was frozen at first. He had no idea what to do. Nothing in his memory prepared him for this. There were no more Cracker Jacks, no more eating; he couldn't move, he wouldn't move. He couldn't breathe, he wouldn't.

His fingers at least were alive. They moved slowly, but with a desperation, across the bottom of the thin box. It was in the corner that they touched it, moved away, then touched it again. Something sharp on an end and hard. Still he did not breathe. More gently than if it were a Cracker Jack, his fingers covered it and tweezed it and slowly pulled the sharp, hard thing from the box. The man knew whatever it was it wasn't for eating, yet such was the habit of his arm that, in one motion, without seeing, he put it to his mouth. Still he did not breathe and the first pain of all those years began to pierce his chest.

He was holding it then not only with his fingers but with his mouth as well. Whatever it was it seemed to fit between his lips. Still he did not breathe and the pain was tearing his lungs loose, making explosions of his heart. Blood filled his face, hot, and water poured from above and within his eyes. He could not breathe, he would not breathe. There was no air. And he knew for the first time in all those years what it was to wish. He wished for air. He wished to breathe.

It was then, at that very moment, that the winds blew out of the four corners of the earth and came rushing to him with a power to shake the world's own lungs away. The winds ran cool over his face and then, with force that staggered him, ran in a thin stream

through whatever he held between his lips
through his mouth and down deep into his
chest. His lungs exploded with a power of their
own and the wind reversed itself and ran
back again from the caverns of his chest. When
at last he breathed, the winds came screaming
infinite loud through the sharp, hard joy
between his lips. A million wings of ecstasy
danced singing out of nowhere and there was
a throng of laughter at his feet. He was on the
highest hill for miles. And the world was
alive and loud at the glorious sound, not of
his breathing but of his blowing. For it was, he
knew at last, the prize; the bird whistle. It
was the sweet taste of childhood.

Theme and Resonating Scripture
Breath of the Lord
Ezekiel 37, 1-14

SMELLS

What mattered least about being the only one
on a tiny planet was how he came to be there.
What mattered more was the smell of the
place, for, he was sure, the planet was once
a mere moving mound of dung. There was
nothing for him to do but sit and hold his
breath for as long as he could. When he had
finally to breathe each time, he did so through
his mouth. The tiny planet, meanwhile, made
its way through the vast nothing of space.

The tiny planet's lone passenger had never
seen such emptiness. Everywhere he looked
was emptiness. There was only the ball of
dung on which he sat, and it was just large
enough for his sitting. It seemed that he and
his smelly little globe had come from nowhere
and were moving rapidly to nowhere again.
It was indeed a solitary feeling and the man
was quite sad. His closest thing to happiness
was in closing off his nose after each whiff
of breath in which he smelled the horrid dung.

Occasionally he thought of simply rolling
off the miserable little planet and in that way
ending the unpleasant life he regrettably
counted as his own. But, for reasons he did
not understand himself, he never did so.
Instead, he continued his disciplined control of
breathing, taking in as little of the horrible
odor as possible. Occasionally he cried. He
did not bawl or sob heavily, but only shed

incidental tears at his lost, lonely and smelly predicament. The small tears fell into a tiny pool between his legs. His crying made matters even worse, for the moisture of his tears on the dung made the odor even stronger.

One day he knew he could go on in that way no longer. He thought again of rolling off the planet, and of bringing his misery to an end in that way. But whatever had kept him from doing that all the times before welled up in him again. Now, however, he experienced the welling up as an immediate knowledge that something new was happening to his dung-world. He sensed that whether he stayed on that moving mound or not was of crucial importance, but he couldn't imagine to whom. But all of this wondering was changing nothing of the horrid odor, and so he put it out of his mind. He decided to leave the dung-planet. He would leave it if even for the dark emptiness of the space around him.

And so it was that the lone passenger stood up, carefully, on the little planet. He would jump, he thought. He would fly free of the smell, the horrid discipline of controlled breathing, free if only for an instant. He poised himself, and felt a trembling step from his feet through his legs to his whole body. He strained his eyes to see another planet in the nothing-space around him—a place for coming from or going to, he didn't care which. But still there was nothing.

He willed himself alert and strong. He would leave the planet of dung—not rolling off as if by accident, but leaping, by clear choice. The moment for his leaping thus had come. Before he could do it, though, he had once more to smell the horrid odor of his home. For the first time in memory, he deliberately unclosed his nose fully. He exhaled all the breath of his lungs, and then, for the first time ever of his time on the dung-planet, he took a long and deep breath. And, oh, the horrid odor was there, nearly knocking him from the planet and depriving him of his leap. But there was something else in the breathing too. A new and second odor, a totally unexpected, unsmelled for odor. Mingled with the smell of dung was the faint but fervent fragrance of April lilac. He quickly exhaled and breathed in again, even more breath this time. It was there again, April lilac sure. In the midst of putrids, odor still, but stronger than the first time. April lilac sure.

He unbraced himself, not thinking of the leap, but of that unexpected fragrance. He looked slowly down at the place on the planet where his tears had always fallen, and he saw it there, one little flower. He saw it there and he breathed in again.

Theme and Resonating Scripture
The Case of Job
Job 42, 1-6. 10-12
63

DEAD ALIVE

He was one specially blessed. From his earliest
days he was a man of precious speech, a
man whose words were wanted everywhere.
Neither his parents nor the neighbors of his
family were surprised at all when he decided,
having come of age, to be a traveling teacher.
On receiving the golden ring of manhood
he said, "I will be a weaver of words and from
this day forward I shall have no home but
wisdom." And so it was that he bid farewell
to his family. They never saw him again.

He journeyed with the sun, carrying no
walking stick, wearing no sandals and having
only one cloak for warmth. On entering a
strange town he would say, "Peace be to this
town." Usually the townspeople, having
heard tales of his wisdom and of his words,
would welcome him with much interest
and respect. If, however, they had not heard of
him or if they were suspicious, he would with
anger shake the dust of their streets from his
feet. His only word then would be the
curse of his farewell.

He moved in this way through many
countries, teaching and sharing wisdom and
words of much wonder. Wherever he spoke
people were filled with the joy that comes of
meeting one whose words are right, and
just enough. Multitudes of people followed

him and tales of his wisdom spread far across the land. He was the one, they said, who could undo the riddles of time. He saw deeply, they said, into the hidden worlds of wishing. Poor and sick and desperate people of every kind came to him and at his word they were somehow enchanted out of misery.

He took great delight at bringing the splendid news of his good words to people so hungry to hear. He loved to have the children near, climbing on his large body. He became their playfulness itself, and laughter from his soul filled more than one valley. It was a remarkable way to live, and it could not last.

The more his fame spread, the more he spoke and the more he offered peace, so much more did people want. They listened to his words ever more closely. They never left him to his silence or to his wisdom's solitude. And the more they wondered at his mystery, the more they sought to find its source. And he himself, too, grew gradually unsettled. He began to seek within himself the fountain of his stunning words. And, strangely, the more he sought, the more he saw that his words were nowhere near as stunning as he and others thought. He spoke to the poor and saw them walk away enchanted, but in their clinging poverty. He spoke to the sick and saw them gladly cooperate in his glib talk of heaven's health. He spoke to dying people and found that his words were wishes of plastic life. He discovered what he thought was so all along. His words to life were cheap talk in a brilliant masquerade of mystery.

One day, in a strange village he had never seen before, he stood in the square by the marketplace and the well. A throng of villagers gathered at the news that he—the one of special word—had come. There was the glad chatter of women, the nervous sounds of expectant joy. The men of the place stood together sharing serious dignity and ready with respect. Children played with a new release, filled with the tone of all the village. There was hope in the air. Soon, as always happened, the people slipped loosely into silence, waiting, watching him. As always, he raised one arm slowly in his gesture of peace. He opened his mouth, but, as never happened before, no word came out. The village followed him from the hope of full silence through a massive loss of voice to the simple hopelessness of having nothing more to say. The teacher, once filled with eloquence, became a stare of wordlessness; his raised arm in peace fell down.

He continued, out of habit and knowing nothing else, to roam the land. However, he roamed now in silence. Soon his followers forgot the promise of his wisdom, the goodness of his news. He became another rootless beggar of no voice at all. A mute. No one noticed when he came into a town and no one noticed when he left. Once on the edge of a village he was seen shaking dust from his sandals, but the villagers laughed at him and imitated his mute, slightly misty stare.

As he grew older and less able to roam without losing the road, he began to yearn more and more for a place of his own. He yearned to be unlooked at, unlaughed at in his wordlessness, unteased by children. His fortune was that, as he grew older, he needed less and less to eat. He needed less and less to beg. So it was that one day he shook the world and its men from his sandals. He lived from then on in a tiny water-place, slightly green, on the edge of a vast desert. He had water enough to drink and dry berries enough to eat. A multitude of seasons passed and they were all as one to him.

One day when he was seated as usual on the edge where the rough green grass met the smooth grain sand of emptiness, he beheld a creature crawling toward him. He watched as a beaten and burned body pulled and pushed itself closer. It was, he saw, a man. He watched as the man crawled past him into the grass and to the small pool of water. He watched as the man drank with hot greed.

After a time he stood and walked to the

pool where the new-come crawler lay. He bent over him and began to wipe the stranger's face with his garment. The stranger said then, "Who are you?"

There was no reply.

Again the stranger spoke. "Tell me, sir, who are you?"

There was no reply.

The stranger lifted himself halfway and grabbed him by the chest of his garment.

"Who are you?" the stranger demanded in a loud voice. "Speak!" he cried. "Can't you speak?"

The only reply was his hard stare of wordlessness.

The newcomer said, "I am dying, can't you see? I am dying for want of a word from another man. I am ages alone. I am dying from being unspoken to. Speak to me!"

There was still no reply but the eyes of the hermit. The stranger fell back to the rough grass, heavier than ever and silent himself for a time.

Then he said, "I see from your eyes that you are dying too, a slower death than mine, but dying too. You are dying for want of a word from yourself. You are ages alone. Your wordlessness is killing me, and I see from your eyes that it is killing you as well." There was silence again as both men sank lower into heat and hopelessness. The sun was gone and the moon was gone and then the newcomer let out a loud groan. The hermit moved closer to him and lifted his upper-body, wiping his face with his garment again. Both men were loud in breathing, though the stranger was slower and heavier. He was less of life even than the hermit.

After a further time, the stranger, still held, said, "A word from you will heal me. A word from you will heal." He said this and held the hermit's eyes. "Do you want me to die?" he asked.

The hermit began then to weep and he lowered his head to rest on the newcomer's neck. From this muffled and muffling place there came a sound. It was a moan from deep in the cave of the hermit's life. But it was a moan that grew clearly into a word. The word was low and long and many times. The word was "No."

Neither man lived through the night. But, when they could have died dead, they died alive.

Theme and Resonating Scripture
Death of Fullness
Luke 2, 25-32

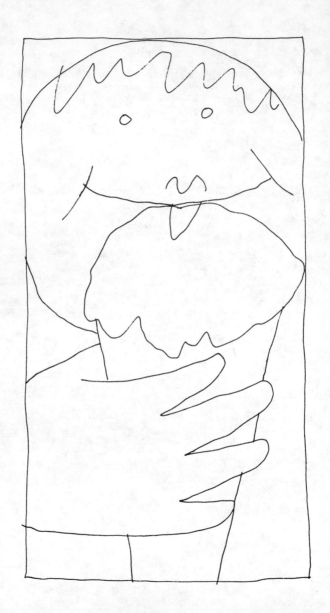

A COMING TO LONG FOR

Only when the day relaxed at evening would
come the marvelous ice cream man. It was
time enough from supper to be hungry again.
It was never too dark, just right for playing
long shadows. It was the time when all the
children were freed on the green to wait, each
one clutching his very own coin for ice. The
boys who lived at the top of the hill would
watch with hard eyes for the slow vanilla
truck, but everyone could listen close for the
jangle of the strawberry bells. Each night
silence settled over the whole green as all the
boys and girls listened. They listened close,
through the last breezes of the leaving day,
through the after-supper chatter of the
whippoorwill. They listened through the very
quiet sound of night and bedtime slipping up
on them. They listened for the final meaning
of the day, for after all the play and laughter,
every child for miles around lived for the
jangle of the strawberry bell and the coming
then of the marvelous ice cream man.

On the evening when this story begins, one
boy in particular waited, listening his very
hardest. His name was William, and of all the
children of the green he was special. He was
special for this: he saw sooner than the other
boys and girls that the delight of the
marvelous ice cream man was a passing joy of

childhood. William saw that the waiting so in silence and the clutching of a coin would not always lead to the great heaven of ice cream bars in all flavors.

So on this evening when William listened, his longing for the strawberry bells was greater than ever. But it was caught halfway by a first-time fear that the bells would never ring and the vanilla truck would never come and the ice cream man would be lost to them all forever.

But it was not so. Oh happily, it was not so. When for the eleventh time, William held his breath vowing not to breathe again until the silence broke, well at that very moment the silence broke at last. There was one sharp, quick jangle of bells in the distance. This was followed by a frozen attention of all the children, trying at once to hear again and know for sure. The boys and girls strained to hear, afraid to look at each other for fear that no one else would have heard that first burst of strawberry. A second time, then, the silence broke. The bells again, muffled less by distance. And then the boys on the hill shouting and waving and jumping like tulips in the wind. The marvelous ice cream man was coming, was coming, was coming again.

And come he did, vanilla truck, licorice wheels and all. And the strawberry bells of course—oh yes, the strawberry bells. They tickled morning out of twilight. What bees and bushes had begun thin sleep jumped awake to hear. Ring-a-ring-a-ding-a-ring. The children exploded like rung bells themselves. They raced, jangling, to the spot where they knew the marvelous ice cream man would stop his vanilla truck.

William was the very last child to arrive at the spot. He was the very last in line. Not that he was usually slower than the other children or less ready with his coin. But William was stunned to hesitation by his gladness at the arrival of the ice cream man, for William alone, remember, had feared for his coming.

All the children cheered when the marvelous ice cream man stepped down from his seat to serve the delights of all flavors. William watched from his place at the rear of the line, feeling slightly bashful and not completely past the fear of before. He saw the other boys and girls with their chocolates and creams and the streamy glee of colors round their mouths. Finally it was his turn, and there William stood, half frozen himself before the big smiling man of all life's ice cream. The man looked down at William and he saw in the boy's eyes something of the fear and something of the hope that made him bashful. And being bashful, William's cheeks went cherry then when the ice cream man shouted to all the children.

"Boys and girls, come back! Gather round for a special prize." All the children came running back, some stumbling to eat and run at once. The ice cream man went on: "It is my privilege, once in my life, to grant to a boy or girl of my choosing whatever wish they harbor deep inside. Because the time is right and because he came to me with wishes in his eyes, I have chosen this boy."

All the children cheered. William was not certain he understood. The ice cream man looked at him then and said, "What is your wish, son, that it might be granted you through me?"

William said nothing for a long time. Slowly he understood what was offered him. His heart pounded in his ears. After a time the ice cream man coaxed him gently: "You have a wish, son?"

And William said, "Yes. I wish that this was a kingdom of all ice cream for everyone forever."

All the children cheered, for they thought this was a fine wish indeed.

The ice cream man, who alone looked suddenly sad, said then, "From this time on it will be so. Be this the ice cream kingdom."

Someone else said, "If it's to be a proper kingdom, we must have a king. Who shall be king?"

Then all the children at once shouted

"William! William!"—for they were very
pleased with his wish. They all continued
cheering for a time, shouting, "Hail, King
William," and "Long live William, king of all
ice cream." By the time they finished shouting
they were all very tired. They all went to
sleep that night without noticing that the
marvelous ice cream man had slipped away.
The next day indeed there was ice cream for
everyone who merely wished for it, endless
ice cream in every flavor. And indeed William
was king of the realm, and, as it turned out,
he was a good and kind king. And all the
children of the green, the ice cream kingdom
now, were happy. The marvelous ice cream
man never came back, for no one would need
to buy ice cream from him. He was never
seen in those parts again, and soon he was
forgotten completely.

Many years went by. They were good years
in which William and his people grew up
together. They grew up with health and full
life because they had the good food of endless
ice cream. But the more that time passed and
the older the people of the kingdom grew,
the more William came to feel that something
in their lives was missing. He couldn't
imagine what that could be, for, because of
his wish, his people had all that they wanted
or needed. They never were bored by their ice
cream or ate so much that sickness came. It

always remained the great delight it is to children, even as they grew.

Still something was missing. William sensed that he and his people had left behind a thing of value. He knew that, if he was yearning for it now, soon all the people of his realm would yearn as well, for they were just like him, though he came to things sooner. Weighed down in this way the king became more and more unhappy, for he loved his people dearly.

One day an old beggar wandered into the realm of all ice cream. Some of the people of the realm found him and, as was the custom, brought him to King William. William always received such beggars with respect and kindness, for he was, as we saw, a goodly king. When the beggar came before William, the king began to ask him the usual questions about name and place of birth and the like. The beggar replied that he was born in a far country and that his name was Jango. William asked the meaning of such a strange name. The beggar replied that he took the name from the sound of his bells.

"Your bells?" the king asked.

"Yes," the beggar replied. "They are in my bundle which I was directed to leave in the outer chamber."

"You carry bells with you?" the king asked.

"Yes. They were part of my trade before.

Even now I shake them as I walk along in the evening."

"What was your trade?" William asked.

The beggar looked hard into William's eyes. Both men were silent for a time.

Then Jango, the old beggar, said: "I was an ice cream man."

"What is that?" the king asked.

"I traded ice cream for coins," replied the beggar.

The king was silent again, looking hard at the beggar. Something missing was moving in him, but he could not find it. He said finally, "How strange. Why would anyone give a coin for ice cream? All one needs is to wish for it."

The beggar said, "It was not always so, sir."

The king thought about that for a moment, but it was late in the day, and so he dismissed the beggar, telling his servant to give him whatever he needed.

A little while later, when the day had begun to relax with evening, the king was strolling on the terrace, heavy of heart as he had come to be. It was then that he heard the servants bid farewell to the beggar in the courtyard below. The king watched the beggar follow the path down the hill. And suddenly, the silence of his heaviness was broken. It was broken by an explosion of bells that brought to

William's mind the taste of strawberry. And all at once a vision of dancing tulips and running laughter washed out of his eyes. The clear cold taste of one waiting ended, of high hope fulfilled, of dearest expectation won again. The clear cold taste of true childhood delighted his very soul. It was a taste far sweeter even than ice cream.

And then King William knew. He knew that the cutting joy of evening was not so much in eating ice cream, but in waiting for the breaking of silence by strawberry bells. He knew that what had been missing from his realm was a coming to long for and listen to. Something to yearn for, or better, a wandering man to love. And so it was that William, young again, ran down the path himself. He found the beggar, embraced him and said, "Will you be a wandering ringer for us of your strawberry bells at evening?"

The beggar, of course, said yes, with a smile of pure vanilla. With cherry glee the king appointed the marvelous ice-cream-man-turned-beggar the evening bell-ringer of the realm.

Theme and Resonating Scripture
Christ's Return
1 Thessalonians 4, 13-18

LILY

I first saw the old man called Shaughnesee
shortly after moving into my writing shack on
the cape, and I saw him then on every day
that remained of his life. It was as if I, his
stranger to the end, had somehow been
charged with his last hard breaths. Perhaps,
feeling so, that is why I went to such lengths
for him at the end. But let me tell you from
the start. Listen carefully, for there is something
elusive about the last days of Shaughnesee.

I had counted myself lucky to find the old
cottage on the high dune overlooking the surf.
It was far enough from town to be isolated
most of the time, even then in summer. It
looked like the perfect place for several
months of hard writing.

On rising the morning after my first night in
the cottage, I went outside to breathe in the
ocean air and the magnificent view. It was
early, perhaps an hour after the sun slipped
out of the far wet horizon. I was surprised and
somewhat disappointed to see a man on the
beach below, perhaps a hundred feet or so
below. I had not expected my lonely sojourn
to be so soon interrupted. I watched the
intruder, jealous of the beach and its solitude.
As he walked slowly along I saw that he was
slightly hunched over and fully clothed.
He wore a long jacket of some kind, though it

was not cold. He wore a hat, a broad-brimmed Stetson like people wore in the late forties. Even from the distance that separated us, I could tell the man was old.

I wondered if he was looking for shells or beach glass, so slow and hunched-over was his walk. But when he came to the spot where the sand was broadest and most clear of rocks, he stopped. I could see then that he carried a stick. He stood facing the ocean, not moving for what seemed a long while. Then he put his stick down and took his hat off. He moved slowly. He carefully placed the hat on the sand. Bending over was an effort for him. He took off the long coat, folded it once, and bent to put it by his hat. He wore a collarless grey shirt that might once have been white. He wore suspenders. Then he picked up the stick again. I thought he must have been very old indeed, so painful did the bending down appear to be.

The old man then began to scratch in the sand with his stick. He seemed to be making random markings on the edge of the water, with a slight push here and a long pull there. Some of the marks were straight lines; others were graceful curves. He never stepped back from the lines as if to get a finer perspective on the whole, nor in any other way did the old man assume the bearing of a knowing artist. Every line seemed to be by whim or accident. Yet, when an hour had passed and the old man walked up the beach and away, he left behind him on the sand a large and delicate flower. From my perch above it seemed to be a lily. An exquisite lily.

That evening I was sitting on the wooden stoop of my cottage watching the ocean go grey with twilight. I hadn't thought of the old man all day. I'd been pleasantly lost in the piece I was doing then. But as evening came and I looked over the beach I remembered the early morning scene. I looked down from the dune. The flower was gone. The tide had come and gone, and with it had gone the exquisite lily. The sand was smooth and unscratched again. Only slight lines of swirled seaweed marked it. Nothing remained of the old man's random tenderness.

I was prepared to remember the incident as one of those pleasant little happenings life gifts us with occasionally, and to let it go, old man, lily and all, at that. But the next morning, at about an hour after sunrise, he returned. He repeated the ritual of hat and coat and, after his hunched-over scratchings, he left another lily in the sand. And so it was the next day, and every day thereafter.

The people in the post office knew the description immediately. Old Shaughnesee, they said, the Irish tinker. He lived in a shack on the coast just down from the Light. Lived alone. Strange one, they said. Never any mail, incoming or out. He traveled the towns around, sharpening knives and fixing kettles and things. An old-time tinker, for sure. Came in handy round here, they said. He'd been doing it for years. Never talked much and no one knew him well. As for the flowers in the sand, they never heard tell of that, neither the post office people nor the man in the pharmacy. Wouldn't be surprised, though. Sounded like something the strange old guy would do.

One grows accustomed to anything. It got so after a month or a little more that I could tell without looking if the old man was down there. I never missed seeing him do the flower. Some days I would sleep later than usual, but I always woke in time to watch the lily take shape. It was as if the flower was as much a part of morning as the sun.

I often wanted to call out to the old fellow or run down and speak to him. But I never did. I don't know why. Afraid, perhaps, of coming between whatever that flower was to him and his silence over it. I thought once of going down to suggest that he draw in the sand farther back from the sea so that the tide wouldn't wash his hard work away. It seemed a shame that the water ruined his lilies as faithfully as he grew them. I didn't suggest it, though. Perhaps he didn't care.

One day late in the summer I did run down from the high dune where my cottage was. I ran with all my heart, half falling all the way. He had just finished his last lily when, instead of going up the beach like always, old Shaughnesee turned and walked into the sea. It took a moment for me to believe he really did it. And then I ran, nearly flew down the dune. I tore across the sand and crashed into the water. I reached him shortly after he went down. There was no struggle. I thought, as I pulled him and dragged him shoreward, that he was already dead. But when we reached the beach he was still breathing. After a moment he opened his eyes. He looked down at the flower and saw that it had been kicked awry and half-ruined. I had torn through it in my rush to get him. He reached his finger out to rescratch a line. Then he looked at me and spoke. "Let me go. Let me go to my lily." And then, just like that, old Shaughnesee died.

I went that day to his shack. I knew without having to decide that I would take him to his family if he had one. I went to his shack to see. I found only some tinker's tools, some old clothes, a rolled-up, battered flag I did not recognize, and a very old photograph of a pretty young girl. There were some papers in a tin box. His name was Brian Shaughnesee, and he was born in Cobh, Ireland. I knew I would take him there.

Later that week, the old man and I flew to Ireland. Cobh, I learned, was a small village in County Killarney on the far southwestern shore. It was cool and misty when we—the old man and I—arrived. I was directed to the mayor's house. When I told him I had brought the body of Brian Shaughnesee for burial, he only looked at me. Finally he said, "Come."

The two of us climbed in the tram, the coffin behind. The mayor directed the driver without speaking. We drove down an old dirt road toward the sea. Finally the mayor said, "Brian was full of zeal during the rebellion years. They made him swear by Holy Mother never to return. His leaving killed his Lily." At that we came down a steep hill to the beach. There was a plot of high ground near the water. An old and weathered tombstone stood alone by the shore. The mayor said, "He'd want to be buried here with her."

As we drew near to the grave I saw that it was surrounded by dozens of exquisite lilies in full bloom. They were the only flowers I saw growing in Cobh. The mayor saw me staring at them, and he said, "Strange. They are always there. It's as if they grow out of the sea for her."

Theme and Resonating Scripture
Faithful Love
Song of Songs 2, 2. 16

SECRET IN HIS DYING

Once upon a time all the people of the realm were terrified. A fierce and mighty dragon, larger even than the king's castle, had been seen within the borders of the land. Many of those who lived there had reported seeing the monster, and one woman said her youngest child had been eaten by it. The woman had gone quite mad with grief.

Everyone was afraid. Of course no one went abroad at night, and every lock was bolted even in the day. The children no longer gathered for their lessons because parents were afraid to send them out. The peasants would go no more alone into the fields for fear that the dragon would see and come. Merchants stopped traveling the roads of the realm, which meant that the goods and spices women loved were not to be had at all. Even the robbers stayed home. The whole realm was terrified.

The king was perplexed. He was a good man as kings went in those days. But he was not known for his abundant wisdom. One day he sat in a meeting with his advisors. His advisors were not known for wisdom either. It was a simple realm with simple people. Until the dragon, in fact, its problems had been simple too. But no longer.

The king said, "We must do something! The

kingdom has come to a stop. The farmers will not farm. The children will not learn. The traders will not trade. Even the robbers will not rob. We must do something!"

One of the advisors, an old lord, said slowly, "Highness, since all you say is true, might I suggest that the ruler at least must rule."

"What?" the king demanded, not understanding.

The lord replied, "Your Highness must do something to rid the kingdom of the dreaded dragon."

"I know that, fool!" the king said. "What I do not know is how to do it."

Another old lord said, "Why not send your noble company of knights?"

The king retorted "You are an even greater fool than he is. **You** are my noble company of knights."

"Oh," said the second lord. "I see the problem."

A third advisor said, "Why not hire some other king's company of noble knights?"

"Good idea," the king said. "But we have no gold with which to pay." The kingdom was not, indeed, a wealthy one.

"I know," said a courtier, who was more sly than the rest. "Let us raise an army from among our own people."

"You mean," the king asked, "the peasants and the merchants and the villagers?"

"Yes, exactly," said the courtier. "If we rally them, their great fear can be turned into soldierly zeal. Even the stoutest of dragons could not withstand a whole army." The courtier was passionate with his plan.

"I don't know," said the king. "They are not a military lot."

"But, Highness," another advisor urged, "with your royal courage to inspire them, they could be a passable army. Even a good one."

"I suppose that is so," said the king. He paused and then went on, "I think what we shall do is raise an army from among our own people. The peasants, the villagers, the merchants. Under my leadership they shall be a great army. Not even the stoutest of dragons shall be able to withstand us."

And so it was that the royal proclamation went forth from the castle to every village, home, and hut in the realm. Every male subject who was neither lame nor too old nor too young was to report immediately for service in the king's great army. It was a royal declaration of war against the dragon. When the people heard this they responded with relief and pride. The dragon would soon regret having come to this land. Nearly every able man in the realm responded immediately and with vigorous enthusiasm. Nearly.

One man did not. Not quite a man, actually. A very young peasant, just old enough to be conscripted, did not leave his humble hut when he heard of the king's command. Instead, he wrote a very courteous letter to the king. In it he explained that, though he appreciated the honor of being invited to join the king's army, he would have to decline. He was, as he explained, a peaceable person. He did not have it in him to bear arms. Not even, he said, against a dragon. He hoped His Highness would understand, and he wished him health and, in conclusion, a long and happy life.

The king, of course, was furious.

"No one," he exclaimed, "shall refuse service in my army. What if everyone felt as this peasant. Why, there would be no royal army at all."

With that the king dispatched a troop of his new soldiers and told them to bring the impudent peasant before him. They did so, roughly. The king was surprised that the peasant was so young, but he remembered that the minimum age for conscription was fairly young. The king stared at the peasant, aware that he was intimidating the lad. Finally he said, "What have you to say for yourself?"

The peasant replied with courtesy, "Your Highness, I tried to say it all in my letter."

But the king said, "Well you didn't. Why do you refuse to bear arms against the dragon?"

The peasant replied, "I cannot bear arms

against any living thing. I am a peaceable man."

"So am I," the king said, "But peace in our realm demands that we bear arms against the evil dragon."

The peasant, who knew little about dragons, simply said, "Your Highness, I am sworn never to bear arms against a living thing."

The king demanded, "Sworn to whom?"

Without hesitating or blushing, the peasant replied, "To my finest fairie."

All the soldiers and advisors who were standing nearby laughed. The king, who was by now greatly disturbed, cried: "Silence!" He then asked the peasant, "To **whom?**"

The peasant replied "To my finest fairie. She is the lady of wisdom who lives in a cave by a stream I know. She showed me in my youth what I know of living things. I have the highest regard for them. I cannot kill a one."

The king did not understand the young peasant at all. Though he seemed a pleasant enough fellow, the king knew only that such refusal, if widespread, would make his great army impossible. So it was that the king, with some reluctance, but with conviction, said to the soldiers nearby, "Take this fellow below and chop his head off." The soldiers did as the king bade them. Never was it known that any other man refused service in the king's great army after that.

What came to be called the war of the dragon went on in the kingdom for a long, long time. The whole realm was devastated by the fighting. The sons of the first soldiers of the king's army were called to serve, so prolonged was the campaign. Strangely, it was not the feared dragon against whom arms were borne. As it turned out, the dragon was never found. The monster was the great threat only for a short time after the first army was called. What happened was this: The soldiers spent the early days of the struggle searching the realm for the dragon. Though he was never located, the soldiers had soon to loose their violence because quarrels among the king's generals broke out. They argued over many things—over whose harvest would be plundered to feed the massive troops, over whose huts would house them, and over other such things. And since the soldiers spent much time in training to fight, it seemed a shame not to let them fight just because there was a scarcity of dragons.

So it was that half the king's army broke away under the generalship of the sly courtier who had first suggested raising the force from among the people of the realm. The courtier in reality wanted to be king. The king in turn, of course, had to defend the honor of his line. Many men died. After many years, it became apparent to everyone, even to the sly courtier and to the king, both of whom were very old, that the war would better be ended. They discovered that wars are easier begun than finished. They did not know how to stop the fighting and killing, which made everyone sad.

One day the courtier and the king came together with their advisors in a truce of sorts.

"How shall we stop the war?" asked the king, for he was still not known for wisdom.

The courtier replied, "I can't think of a way to stop it, Highness."

An old advisor to the king spoke then: "Sirs, I heard once somewhere of a lady of wisdom, a river fairie, who lives by a stream. Perhaps if we found her she could tell us how to stop the war."

"Yes," they all said. The king and the courtier sent their men searching, and soon the cave of the fairie was located deep in the hills and truly by a stream.

The king and the courtier gathered at the cave with their advisors. They called to the fairie and waited. After a long time a beautiful maid with golden hair and spun gowns appeared before them.

"What do you seek?" she asked.

"O Lady of Wisdom," the king said, "we seek to know how to stop the wars we began."

The fairie replied, "I have given that secret away already. It was mine for the giving only once. You must ask him to whom I gave the secret."

"Who is he," the courtier asked, "that we might ask him?"

The lady replied, "He was a young peasant years ago. A peaceable man. He swore allegiance to me, to live truly by the secret I gave him. I do not know his name."

The courtier spoke quickly then, "I know of whom she speaks." He turned to the king. "She speaks of the peasant you put to death, the man who would not bear arms against the dragon."

The king thought deeply at this. He had never forgotten the young peasant of his past.

The courtier continued, angry now and drawing his sword at the king. "He had the secret, you fool, and you put him to death. Now we shall never have it."

The king looked at the courtier. He too drew his sword. "For once, sir, you are wrong. The peasant gave us his secret, though we did not see it. He gave us the secret of living in his dying." And with that the king dropped his sword to the ground and slowly walked away.

Theme and Resonating Scripture
Revelation of Death
Luke 23, 44-49

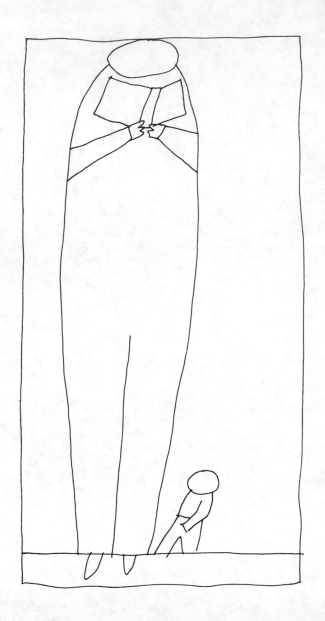

DUMB GIANT TOM

Tom, the dumb giant, could not read. One day
he was walking through the forest near his
house. He did not own the forest, though he
thought of it as his own. He was large enough
to own it if owning was arguing. He was
the biggest man in all the land. But he was
also very shy. He was so timid that the rabbits
of the forest played games of teasing him.

As he walked along a squirrel squeaked up
at him, "Hey Tom, will it rain today?"

Though he was startled at first, the giant
nodded hello, and stretched himself up to
his full height, brushing through the branches
of the trees. He looked at the sky. It was blue.

"No," he replied, "probably not. It's dry
up here."

The squirrel thanked him and ran off.

Just then the fox came by and said, "Hey,
big fellow, which way to the river?"

Tom said, " I don't know."

To which the fox replied, "Well stretch that
monster frame of yours and look for it."

The fox spoke this way because Tom's
timidity was well known in the forest.

Tom looked over the trees. He couldn't see
the river. He said to the fox, "I don't see no
river."

The fox replied angrily, "Look again and
find it or I'll bite your foot."

The fox was, you see, very good at coaxing people to do things his way. Tom stretched up taller than ever and strained his eyes and in this way finally saw the river. He pointed the way for the fox, who went on without even so much as a thank you.

As Tom went on his way he was very angry at the fox, and that's why he pushed the branches out of his way with extra-hard force. The leaves of the branches began to protest, shouting together, "Hey Tom, cut it out; you're breaking us." Well Tom didn't want to break anybody, so he stopped pushing the branches with such force. Indeed he stopped walking altogether and sat down on a low hill.

From his place on the low hill Tom could see the school house in the clearing. He had gone to school there once himself years before, but only for a short time. The other children had laughed so hard at him because of his size that he quit. His mother had not wanted him to quit, but she gave in when he insisted. Tom did not have a father, so there was no argument from him. As he sat on the low hill this day, he wondered what they were doing in the school house.

Just then a little boy appeared from behind the bushes. "Hi, Tom," he said. "What are you doing here by the school house?"

"Hi there, boy." Tom wanted the child to

think he was just resting. "I'm just resting," Tom said, and then asked: "What are you doing out here?"

The boy said, "It's reading time. Teacher lets us read outside if we want to."

Tom asked, "What you gonna read?"

"My book," the boy answered, holding it up for Tom to see.

"Oh yea," Tom said, "looks like a good one." Though he said this he had no idea what the cover of the book said, for, remember, he could not read.

"Hey Tom," the boy said, "can I practice my reading with you?"

"Sure," Tom said, hoping the boy would not need his help or discover his ignorance.

The boy began to read, slowly and with difficulty: "A Golden Treasure Book. The Story of Jack and the Beanstalk."

As the boy began to read the story, Tom grew intensely interested, for there was in the story a giant who lived in a castle on the clouds. The little boy read one slow word at a time. A strange feeling settled over Tom. He had no sooner recognized the picture of the giant and the description of the castle than the little boy stood up and ran toward the school house. He shouted over his shoulder, "Time for rest period, Tom. I'll see you tomorrow." Tom was slightly dazed, for something in him had recognized the giant in the story as the father he had never known.

Every day Tom returned to the low hill on the edge of the clearing that held the school house. Every day he walked the familiar trail through the forest he thought of as his own. He passed the teasing rabbits and the mean fox and the nervous leaves. Every day he noticed less and less of their world. He had slowly been wooed by the world of Jack and the beanstalk.

There was a gradual building of terror about the little boy's story. Tom knew that he was learning at last about his own daddy. His mother had often told him about the castle in the clouds and the goose that laid golden eggs and that it was all lost somehow. Tom had never known how and now he was learning. Every day at reading time he learned.

The little boy was reading and Tom, as always, listened very closely. The little boy pointed his finger at each word.

"Jack had found at last the key to the room where the golden goose was kept. More quickly than clouds, he had the goose and ran from the castle. As he ran down the long vapor stairs of the giant's home he heard the rumbling of the great giant stirring and leaving his huge bed for the chase. Jack ran as fast as his legs would carry him. He heard the giant roar, 'Fee, Fi, Fo, Fum,' and heard the giant running after him. Jack leapt on the beanstalk and, balancing the goose, climbed down quickly. The giant, mean and angry, was right behind him.

The little boy stopped reading. Tom, who was hardly breathing, said, "It's not time yet. Keep reading! Please."

The little boy said, "Tom, I can't. I'm frightened." And then, handing the book up to the giant said, "Here, you finish it."

Tom took the book. He didn't want the boy to know he couldn't read. And, for some reason, he didn't want the boy to know of his heart's great beating. He looked mutely at the book. There was a picture of a boy chopping down a big vine with an axe, and on the next page a picture of a giant falling. There were words below the pictures, but Tom looked mainly at the pictures.

He began to speak, slowly and carefully, as if reading. "Jack reached the ground, and, because he was afraid of the giant, he took an axe and chopped the beanstalk down. The vine fell from the sky and the giant fell too. He fell down hard and hurt himself when he hit. He hurt himself bad. He was all lying in a heap on the ground and Jack went over to him. Jack still had the goose he stole from the poor giant. The poor giant, said to Jack, Jack you needn't oughta done that. I weren't gonna hurt ya.'"

Tom's eyes overflowed with tears. He

continued to speak, looking at the book. He never turned a page. He was speaking faster and less carefully.

"'I were gonna tell ya you could have that old goose there. I don't need it no more. I got my little boy Tommy to keep me happy. That old goose you can have.' And then that big old giant, he died. And Jack, that giant killer, he cried. And that's the end of the story, little boy."

"Tom," the little boy said, "you read real good."

"Yea," Tom said, clutching the book.

He was kind of smiling in a new way for him. "Them words come out like golden eggs."

Theme and Resonating Scripture
Dreams and Wishes
Acts 2, 14-18; Job 33, 14-15; Joel 2, 28-29

NIGHT RIVER BANK

It was, in a way, Nickie's very first night of
deep wondering. He was outdoors, by the river
that ran through the city. It was late, later
than he'd ever been out alone before. Because
of this, because it made him at once happy
with adventure and somewhat afraid, he ran by
the river. He ran in short, quick spurts of
wind that were calculated to, at once,
heighten adventure and temper fear. Nickie
was, you see, a little boy.

He ran as far as the children's waterside
park, the low-fenced place for playing in the
afternoon. Nickie stopped running and
looked at the playground. The boards hung
by chains for swinging on, the high metal hill
for sliding down, the worn cage for climbing
in and out of—it was all there. But alone
and unused except by night's shadow, it was
not the familiar place of laughter and light. It
was a place, suddenly, of fear.

Nickie ran on, a new spurt of wind with him.
He flew a bit, a quick, darting jet-plane. But
only a bit, flying quick and free. He
remembered why and where the running—
remembered and knew he'd known all the
running long. He was running to the water to
investigate, to look a little at what he called
the night river bank.

The night river bank was not the edge of the

river but the river itself. The night river bank was the gold hoard of coins piled deep below the lights of the city. He could see the piles, something like stacks of new pennies, from his own room's window at home. Every night he would look out at the black river and see a king's treasure shimmering under the shadow of buildings and bridges and tall unknowns. Every night he would say to himself, "I'll find out sometime about the treasure. I'll learn the way in to that night river bank over there." On this night of his running, Nickie left his house after his parents went to bed. He left his house to learn.

Nickie ran until he came to where the grass met the water with small rocks. He had left his house, his parents, his playground—almost everything, in fact—behind. He stood still, looking out at what alone was left—the night river bank of piled, quilted pennies. It was his moment of deep wondering. And such a moment was it that he was not frightened when the silence was coaxed apart by an old man's voice.

"Hello, child." Nickie turned and saw a pair of easy eyes. They were at the same level as his own. The man was sitting on the grass by the water. He had been there all along, throughout the time of wondering and of silence. The man's voice had been old, and then Nickie could see his face and see that it, too, was old. Very old. He was the first very old man who had ever spoken to him. He spoke again. "Child, what are you doing out here alone?"

Nickie said nothing. He only looked at the old man. He reminded him of someone's grandfather, maybe his own grandfather whom he could not remember. Nickie still was not afraid. The old man repeated his question. "Child, what are you doing out here alone?" And Nickie said "I have come to see the night river bank up close."

"Ah," said the old man, "The night river bank. You mean, I suppose, the reflections of the city lights on the water?"

"No," Nickie replied, "The golden piles there, like new pennies in the water."

"Ah, good," said the old man. "I was not sure you'd come for that. I was not sure you'd seen the treasure in the deep. Well, now that you're here up close, what do you think of it all?"

Nickie thought for a moment and then said, "How does somebody get into it, the night river bank?"

The old man said, "Oh, child, you need not worry on that. It's a question answered soon enough."

Nickie didn't understand that. He asked another question. "What is it like, the deep treasure place?"

"You must think of it, child, as the fish do. Make a picture in your mind of how the city lights look to them. It is a world down below of jewels hanging from the sky. There are a million needle-thin shafts of brilliance to flash your skin with, to make messages of light for all your friends to see.

"It's a kingdom there where everyone is king. The coins piled deep, the ones you see from here, are the treasure of that world. It's a treasure for everyone, and so no one needs to buy or sell. It's all giving presents there. So it is that the coins are always piled, gold and neat as you see tonight.

"And child, the river treasure deep is a world for such as you. It is not of our time below. It is of the very childhood of time. The place of the kingdom where fish and others live is what it was everywhere before the beginning began. There is no age, but youth, no growing but to simplicity, no old or being old. . . ."

Nickie interrupted, "But you are old. How do you know all this if you are old?"

"I am old," the old man said, "because I am here. If I was there I would be younger even than you."

"Why," Nickie asked, "are you here, then?"

"I am here," replied the man, "for you. I am here for the ones with whom you play on that place of play back there. I am here to

112

collect the treasure the city steals and throws away. I pick it up and tend it for the night river bank."

"What does the city steal?" Nickie wanted to know.

"The city steals childhood from children. It steals it in a thousand little ways, and when the children have no childhood left they forget what is gone and become grownup people. The city, having stolen childhood, has no use for it and throws it away. I wait here by the children's park and by the river at night. I gather the treasure up and tend it. It is the treasure of play and playfulness, and laughter over nothing in particular, and afternoon naps, and littleness in general."

"What," Nickie asked, "do you do with it all?"

"I do what all wealthy fools do. I cherish for a time and, finally, I deposit it. I deposit the gold of stolen childhood in, as you said yourself, the night river bank. That's why the piles of gold in black water grow a little bit bigger each night. Each night a little castoff wondering is added to the stack and a little bit of childhood begins a deep down eternity of hide and seek."

Nickie asked then, "But, if you can see the treasure at night, see it even grow, why don't grownups come and get some too?"

"They do at times, child, in a way. But

113

mainly the piles of pennies are just a hint for
them to be noticed now and then of the
treasure at the deep of the world. As the piles
grow and grow the hint will be once clear
enough and noticed enough so that the deep
river bank won't be hoarding the treasure
anymore. Everyone, childhood or no,
will know."

Nickie said then, "But, sir, if I know now,
why do I have to wait? I want it now."

"Yes, child," the old man said. "And well
you should. And so you came tonight. You are
what has been stolen from a lad named
Nicholas. He sleeps tonight and will for a time
to come. But now, Nickie, you may play.
You may, by playing, make the hint higher
for him and others."

"Sir, how will this happen? How will the
treasure be mine?"

"The treasure is already in you, child, and it
happens so: put your hand in mine; let your
fingers dance in tickling me. Now my turn
tickling you. And, that's it, good! It happens,
you see, by laughing a little."

Theme and Resonating Scripture
Crossing Over
Exodus 14, 15-31

114

LEGS

"Hey, Stevie, you asleep?"

"Yea, why?"

"Just saying good night."

"O.K., good night, baby brother."

"Ha Ha."

Steve smiled to himself. His brother Mark didn't like it when he called him "baby brother," but it had become their nighttime joke. It was o.k. to say it just before going to sleep. Once said, they could roll over in their beds, crunch their pillows and slip under silence.

The moment of good night was a strange one for Steve. It was always, nearly every night, a time when he, twelve and the older, really and truly liked Mark, who was only ten. Most other times they hated each other, sometimes even fighting, fists and all.

It was in the fighting that Steve hated Mark most because the younger brother had an advantage that made their matches unbearable. Mark could run. Steve, long lame from polio, could not. He could stand and walk in his own slow way. But he could not run. When fights broke out, Steve could punch harder and squeeze tighter, but Mark could hit and run. That was when Steve hated him the most.

But not at night, just before sleep. On this night Steve felt the old love. He pushed it aside, maybe blushing in the dark.

Soon Steve was on the edge of the great forest that sleep took him to sometimes. It was a deep and primeval wood with low mist always, and a silence that stopped everything. It was a place of great mystery. Steve had explored the forest during the sleep of other nights. He knew somehow that the place had secrets to give and he had not found them yet. So it was that on this night he set out again to wander the strange woods. His eyes were sharper than ever, though the shadows were deep and hidden. Steve followed the path he had used before, conscious of the noise of his clumsy, limping walk. He dragged his right foot slightly, and it left his crippled mark in the dirt.

The boy wandered his way deep into the forest. He was alert and looking, but not afraid exactly. Some of what he saw was familiar to him from other nights: a certain dark brook, an old arching oak, the sounds of quick animal things. But on this night there was something new. He was, first of all, deeper into the wood than he had ever been. This is why, perhaps, there was more mystery than ever in the air. He had a new feeling that something especially strange was coming, that the night for the secrets maybe had come.

And so it turned out to be. After dragging his foot for a long time, Steve came to a large opening in a big rock wall. It was like a cave. It was, he saw on moving slowly closer, a cave indeed. He stopped and stood still, looking through the opening, straining his eyes to see what was there. He saw nothing. He took a deep breath, summoned his courage and moved slowly, noisily with his limp, into the cave.

Oh, it was dark and cold. He walked for what seemed hours but wasn't. Finally he came to a big, hall-like cavern. A small fire was burning in its center and he was enabled to see. He thought he was alone at first, but, of course, he wasn't. A man wearing a long robe stepped out of the shadows behind him. Steve was startled, and for the first time that night he was truly frightened. The man spoke.

"You've come, have you?"

It was as if he'd been expected. Steve said nothing.

"Well," the man continued, "let's be about it."

Steve did not understand, and so he asked, "Be about what?"

"Your wish, of course. You do have a wish, don't you?"

Steve replied, "I don't know. Who are you?"

The man said, "I assumed you knew, or would guess it at least. I am the warlock of the woods. Any man who finds his way to this my cavern is entitled to one fulfilled wish.

One request, you understand?"

Steve was still mystified. "You mean anything I want?"

"Yes," the warlock replied. "But once only."

"Oh," Steve said.

"What will it be?"

Steve understood now, and he nearly trembled that this was indeed true. He didn't need more than a second or two to know what his wish would be.

"I wish that I had good legs to run fast with."

The warlock's eyes fell quickly, almost unnoticeably, to Steve's legs. Steve noticed however, and he shifted his weight. He waited. Finally the warlock said,

"All right. That shouldn't be too difficult. Are you ready for quick moving?"

Before Steve could reply, the warlock had thrown part of his long robe around him and everything had gone quite black. For an instant only Steve closed his eyes.

When he opened them, he was startled to see after quick blinking that he was in his own room, laying still in his own bed. He half smiled at himself. So it had only been a dream. But then, out of the shadow by the closet, there stepped the warlock once again.

Steve was quite confused now and said, "What are we doing here?"

The warlock replied, "We have come to fix your legs. Lie back and relax. This will take a little time."

"What will?" Steve asked.

"The transference."

"What's that?"

"The cellular transference of his legs to yours." When he said this, the warlock nodded in the direction of the room's other bed. Mark was hard asleep. Steve looked over at Mark. Then he whispered, "Of his legs to mine? But what about him?"

"Oh," the warlock replied, "don't worry about that. The transference is dual. He will have your legs."

"Oh, no!" cried Steve. "I mean I never thought it would be like that."

The warlock was impatient. "Did you think I could pull a pair of healthy legs for fast running out of the air? They must be had, my boy. Now relax."

"No." Steve said. "I don't want it like that." He thought of Mark, of **his** limping, dragging **his** foot.

But the warlock said, "No one will ever know. They will think it was always so."

"No," Steve said. "I've changed my mind."

"Sorry," said the warlock. "It's too late. It's done. Good night."

And with that, the long-robed stranger was gone. Steve felt a frenzy of never before. He threw the blankets off his body and looked down at his legs. He couldn't tell. He sat up and turned in bed, dropping his legs over

the side. He stood and then he did not move.
He felt quite different. He picked his right
foot up. The toes were straight; the ankle was
not twisted. He put it down and lifted the left.
Then he began to lift and drop both legs in
turn, slowly at first, then fast. He was, Oh God,
running in place. A swell of joy and
exhilaration came over Steve. His legs were
whole. He could run. Oh, God!

But then Steve saw Mark. He saw the form
of his brother's legs beneath the blanket.
Carefully he lifted the far edge of the wool
and, not breathing, he looked. The very
familiar feet, bony; the shins, too skinny; the
bumpy knees. His legs of all these years were
there in his brother's bed, on Mark's body.
Oh God! No.

And so it was that Steve set out again that
night for the dark, primeval forest. But with
this difference. He ran! He ran all the way. He
ran faster than any bird could fly. He leapt
over fallen, moss-covered logs. He screeched
down hills into deep hollows, jumping, flying,
quick and light as a jungle cat. He swung
around trees to slow for turns and he kicked
up more leaves than autumn sees. Several
times he fell, cutting his knees enough to color
them with red patches. But he was up, not
noticing, off again. He was running, running,
for the forest, for the cave, but most of all
for Mark.

But Steve could not find the cave. His

quick legs were of no use in that. Winded after
an age of running, he stopped and sat on the
stump of a tree. He was trying to catch his
breath, wondering what in the world to do,
when, looking down at the ground, he saw
them. He saw tracks in the dirt, the tracks in
the dirt of a cripple. They were unmistakable,
with their long drag marks and turned out
prints of feet. Steve stood and turned and
followed the marks of old familiar legs. Within
a short time, he was in front of the large
cave. He smiled when he thought of his
coming; all the running in the world would
have led nowhere. It was the tracks of his very
own legs, slow but efficient, that brought
about wishing again.

The warlock had never been bothered with
wishes twice in the same year, much less twice
in the same night, so hidden was his cavern
in the cave of the wood. So it was that with
the coming of morning that night, only the
warlock and Mark still suffered. The first from
lack of sleep and the second from strange
scratches on his knees. When Mark showed
the bruises to his brother, Steve only laughed,
saying that he himself, by never running,
had never cut a knee. So there, baby brother.
Ha. Ha.

Theme and Resonating Scripture
Brothers' Love
1 John 3, 1-2. 16-19

123

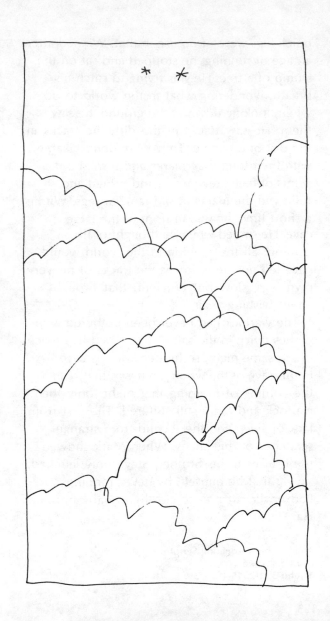

HEAVEN?

Two purple dragonflies were sitting in a curled
dry leaf in the middle of a large pond one
day. Their conversation went like this:

"Do you believe in heaven?"

"Yes, I suppose so. Why? Don't you?"

"I'm not sure at all. Can you take me there?"

"Well, they say it's up above. Perhaps we
   could fly on up."

"Let's do. Come on. Show me the way."

And so the two dragonflies set out one day
to fly their way to heaven. They had no idea
where heaven was, except they'd always
heard it was up above. So up above they flew.
Very quickly they were up above the trees.
They hovered there and their conversation
went like this:

"I don't see it, do you?"

"No. Though the pond down there is lovely,
isn't it?"

They flew on, then. The rapid fluttering of
their tiny wings carried them high above
the country. They paused in their climbing.
They could see all the way to the far hills of
blue. Their conversation went like this:

"I don't see it, do you?"

"No. I don't see anything that looks like
heaven should. But what a lovely view."

"How much higher must we fly?"

"I don't know. Why? Are you tired?"

"Yes, very."

"Well, perhaps above the clouds there."

And so they fluttered on. It took longer to reach the clouds than either of them thought. Both were disappointed to find no sign of heaven even there. And both by then were quite tired. They rested on the clouds, and their conversation went like this:

"If heaven isn't here, perhaps it isn't anywhere. Shall we go back?"

"No, not now. We've come too far."

"But it is so very difficult and it may all in the end be for nothing."

"But to go back now is to go back with no heaven to believe in. What could we put in its place."

"I suppose. But, well, up above is a long, long way from here."

And so it was. Nevertheless the two dragonflies set out again. They flew from then on in the cooperative way peculiar to dragonflies, with their long tails attached. In this way, they were able to preserve their energy, and though flying was slower, they increased their range manyfold.

Their upward fluttering took them to the regions of very thin air, the final edge of earth-atmosphere. Even there no sign of heaven appeared. So they braced themselves and gathered all their speed and plunged out into space. The darkness frightened the two dragonflies, but soon they became accustomed to it and could see quite well. The earth fizzled behind them like a blue balloon slowly losing its air. They moved farther and farther out into the black reaches of nothing.

After quite a long stretch of flying they came to the earth's moon. The two dragonflies, flying as one still, landed there to rest. The terrain was barren and cold, quite clearly nothing of heaven. Their conversation went like this:

"You know, I could still accept that heaven is somewhere up above. My problem right now is in trying to figure which way up above has come to be."

"That's so. If we went straight up from here, we'd be back on the earth."

"True. Which must mean up above is the other way."

"Good thinking."

So they set out the other way. Their journey took them farther and farther into the dark hole that space seemed to be. They brushed by small bits of rock that floated freely here and there. They held fast to each other, for the farther they went the more empty and fearful their flight became.

They passed several minor planets. They could tell without landing that none of them was heaven. They all had the hard grey dullness that was coming to seem common.

The two dragonflies rested for a while on one of Jupiter's moons and then moved on. They traveled for a long, long time, seeing nothing but occasional floating bits of rock. One day their conversation went like this:

"You know, I think this may have been a mistake."

"I'm afraid you're right. Heaven-seeking is turning out to be just plain hellish, isn't it?"

"Do you think we are through?"

"Well now, there's nothing left to do but push on. We'd never find our way back anyway."

"But do you still believe in heaven?"

"What else is there?"

"There's earth."

"The two have become the same for me."

"Me too."

The dragonflies pushed on. They grew old in the journey through space. After a while they forgot about heaven and simply, from force of habit, pushed on. And they stopped talking to each other. They stopped having conversations. It was then that the space through which they flew became truly empty. It got so that neither dragonfly was sure that life was still in him. Both were numb. They might have been dead.

But, in fact, they were not. They were alive. But after their long, long journey of stupor, they were far from alert. Which, at a certain point, became a special shame, because out of the black appeared suddenly a beautiful planet of abundant life and color. The two dragonflies did not experience their drawing near to it. They felt no anticipation as they gradually were tugged by strange, but gentle, forces. They were tugged toward the incredibly beautiful planet that lay below them, or above them. It was not clear which, nor was it important.

The dragonflies became slowly aware of the new world spread before them. They were no longer in control of their flying. And their attention soon was completely taken up by the world of their approach. They were mixes of fear and awe and new hope. Even after traveling through the whole universe, neither had ever seen such beauty. Their approach was slow as they came close to the place. Magnificent vistas stretched before them. Trees and far hills of blue. There was a peace about the place and though it was strange and foreign, it felt in a way like home.

Soon the joined pair were level with trees. They held tightly to each other as they neared the surface of the place. It was a beautiful silver plain that waited to welcome them. It glistened with gold and sparkling jewels, yet was, it could be seen, soft and easy. The forces pulling the dragonflies settled them carefully in a comfortable and pleasant hollow cushion of some kind. They were at rest for the first time in a cosmos' age.

They still held tight to each other as they looked around. They saw quick birds of beauty and a caressing hill of trees. They saw banks of orange flowers and caretaking bees. They heard the welcome call of whippoorwill and the laughter of April springs. Then they saw that the silver plain of their welcome was a large pond and they saw that their new cushion was an old curled leaf afloat.

They looked at each other and laughed. The two dragonflies spoke for the first time in memory and their conversation went like this:

"Heaven?"

"Hell, yes."

Theme and Resonating Scripture
The Place of Rest
Hebrews 4, 1-10

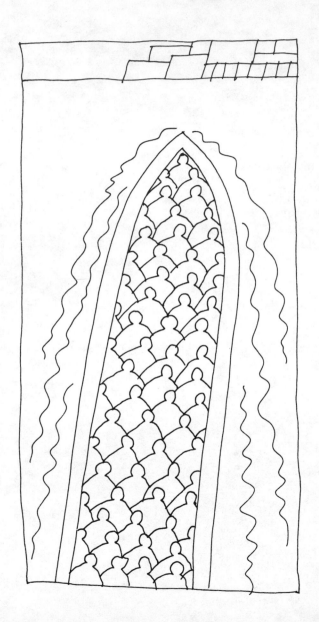

THE BARGE PEOPLE

The city was sleeping when the large river
barge crawled quietly into the night. No one
noticed the arrival of the boat, and certainly no
one noticed that night that it was a river
vessel unlike any other. It was long and narrow
like the others. It was flat bottomed like the
others for passing through the low locks and
shallow canals of the inland waterways. Like
many other barges it had a narrow pointed
prow for ocean travel. It was moving
south with the river current toward the sea
when it pulled quietly into the sleeping city.

Though this particular river barge looked
like any other, it was in fact unique. What
made it so was this: other barges carry much
cargo and a few people. This one carried a
little cargo, mainly food, and many people.
They were young and old, men and women,
lighthearted and down, strange and very
ordinary. They lived on the barge and in it, on
the flat deck with blankets only, in the cabins
below if it rained. Mainly, though, they lived
in the lives of each other. They were the
barge people.

The morning after they arrived some of the
barge people went into the city. The city itself
still had not taken note of the vessel, for
many barges stopped there on the way to the
sea. Some of the barge people went to the

stores of the city to buy food and drink for all the rest. But the others who went ashore scattered in the city. They wandered down the back streets of the place. They went into the dark corners of the place. And they all did the same thing. When one of the barge people saw a man lying in the back street, or a man looking for food in the cans of garbage, or a man with a lost light in his eye, he would approach and say, "Hello, I'm just off the barge on the river. We could use you to replace a man who's leaving us today. We are going to the sea."

Invariably, because of the way it was said and because of the sea, the poor or the hungry or lost man would lift himself up and nod in some way and follow. And so it was that by noon of the day after the night they had come into the city the barge people who had gone ashore returned. Each brought one of the back-street people with him. Each of the city people was shown his sleeping place, given something to eat and told about the voyage to the beautiful sea. All of this was done by the person from the barge who had invited him aboard.

When dusk was near and the barge was about to move on, everyone gathered on the deck. The barge people who had gone into the city that morning began to say farewell to the other barge people. The city people came to understand that their special hosts, the ones who'd found them and brought them back, were leaving the barge, would not go on to the sea. One of the back-street people, an old man who was sick, approached one of the barge people and asked why the others were leaving. He was told that there was not room enough for them to stay. They had to remain in the city. The old man objected and said that in such a case the city people should be the ones to leave. He was told that the barge had come to the city for them, and that the barge people wanted it so. The old man said then that the sea and hoping for it was too precious, and they should be able to get there. But the barge person to whom he objected said only, "Yes, but perhaps there will be another barge to the sea for them someday."

And so it was that the strange vessel moved on in the current of the river, with its cargo of people, some of the city, and some, of course, of the barge itself. The back-street people grew more and more enchanted by their barge-vision of the sea. They yearned for the open space of unbroken horizons. They craved the blue stretch of air without poison. They longed for the silence of sea gulls only and waves. Every day the city people grew more and more to love the barge, its people and the hope it had given them.

As the barge flowed its way toward the sea, it passed through several other cities. At each one, the vessel stopped. At each one, some of the barge people went ashore for food and drink. At each one some of the barge people went ashore for the lost ones of the city. The exchange of the first ashore was repeated again and again, so that, as the barge moved closer to the sea, there were fewer and fewer barge people and more and more back-street people of the cities. And each time that the barge moved on, someone told a worried newcomer, "Perhaps there will be another barge to the sea for them someday."

One morning, after a long time and much thick water had passed, a gull appeared above the barge, then two, then many. The sea at last was near. The word passed quickly through the vessel, over its deck and through all its cabins. The people rushed to the open surface of the barge. They were alive with laughter and excitement. They would live through a wish fulfilled at last. As the barge rounded a final turn in the river, the rich blue of ocean broke into the muddy water ahead. The barge was moving with the current into the mouth of the river. The river was pouring itself out into freedom.

An old man who came from a back street of the first city was the first of the people to notice. He saw that there was an inland waterway channel to the left ahead, and he was looking for the barge man on the tiller. He wanted to watch the turning out to sea. But there was no barge man on the tiller. The old man looked across the crowd and saw that there was no barge man anywhere on the barge. The barge people were gone. Only the back-street people remained.

The old man screamed, his voice shrill and sudden and more alive than he was. The back-street people were stunned. They turned from looking at the ocean to look at him. No one spoke. The old man moved his eyes again across the crowd, to the inland channel ahead, back across the crowd and to the tiller. Still no one spoke. The back-street people turned toward the sea again. The barge was moving away from the last inland channel.

Still no one spoke. Each of the people thought of the sea, of his city of before, of the barge person in whose place he slept, and of the empty-handed tiller behind. At that moment, just a short time after the old man screamed, all the back-street people moved slowly and together to the left side of the barge. Such a delicate shifting of weight was it that the strange vessel itself turned slightly to the left. Not much of a turn. Just enough to turn the barge inland again to the cities instead of the sea. Not much of a turn. Just enough to turn the back-street crowd into barge people.

Theme and Resonating Scripture
Community of Love
John 17, 18-24

NOBLES THREE

Once, not so very long ago, the large Eastern desert of the earth was commonly considered to be the devil's haunt. It was an endless heap of limestone hills, bare and blistered, now rising and falling with monotonous laziness, now cut sharply in sections by dark ravines. Harsh and constant winds swirled over the region with a high fury that some said was Satan's whistle. Animals, oxen, or sheep that wandered by mistake into the place were never seen again. Some said they were lost to thirst in the sun; some said they were lost to the king of all evil himself. No one knew for certain because no owner of an animal would pursue his beast into that dreaded place.

The devil was said to take many forms, all of them monstrous. He appeared, they said, as a python, as a huge roaring dragon, as a winged lizard that flew from shadows. He was able, it was said, to cast a spell that would forever make a captive of a man, and he was waiting always in the desert for a man over whom to throw it. It was unclear, though, how people came to know so much about the hidden monster, since, as far as anyone could tell, no one had ever ventured into the desert alone.

No one, that is, until the nobles three came

139

along. The nobles three were strong and honest knights who went from realm to realm doing good. They were known as fierce friends to kings and common folk alike. It so happened one day that the three nobles came to a village near the edge of the great fearful desert. They saw that it was a poor village, growing poorer. People were fleeing it because it was too near the devil's desert. When the three nobles heard this they were moved with compassion. They had long heard of the hidden beast of the wasted land, and, after conferring for a short time, they announced they would slay him.

The people rejoiced. If anyone could conquer the enemy, these three pure and courageous knights could do so. The knights agreed. After obtaining what they needed, they entered the hot and empty desert. One of the three was expert with the combat net, and he carried that alone. A second was armed with his long fighting pole. It was said that he could subdue a mighty bear with it and nothing else. The third noble carried no weapons, for he was the bearer of the strongest body anyone had ever seen. Besides these strengths, the three nobles brought with them a huge, high-walled cart. It was drawn by eight of the best draught horses in the land. The huge wagon was for bringing the vanquished devil home in.

So it was that the unwalked ravines and unseen limestone hills were walked upon and seen by men for the first time ever in memory. The three nobles were diligent in their search. They slept little, moving continuously through the heat of hard days and the cold of quick nights. But many moons turned, and they found no sign of the hidden beast. There were small rodents and little snakes, but no pythons. There were huge fallen trees, but no dragons. There were countless screaming vultures, but no winged lizards. On most days there wasn't even the high whistle of the wind.

The nobles three began to wonder if they were alone in the vast desert. Never in their long journeys had they experienced such bitter disappointment. There were no beasts whatever to be vanquished. There was only the vanquishing sun and thirst. Eventually the wagon horses became testy and impatient. And, eventually, so did the three nobles. They began to argue about which trails to follow, which birds to track, which shades to rest in. Their arguing grew fiercer and fiercer and more constant.

One day each of the three nobles began his own private hoard of water, each holding back from the common skin. On that very day—in fact, at that very moment—their bickerings were interrupted by the furious, unexpected assault of the hidden beast. Out of nowhere Satan was on them, tearing, growling, burning, screeching. All three of the nobles were stunned, but quickly they recovered. They were glad to unleash their strength in combat once again. And they needed all they had. The desert devil was python, dragon, winged lizard all in one. It was the struggle of their lives, each grappling with part of the enemy. Net, pole and muscles strained. The three nobles pulled all their past victories together in one massive effort. After a long, long time of such furious combat, they felt the beast yielding, losing strength, gasping. They moved the failing devil toward the huge cart, and with one final frenzy they forced him over the high walls and into the wagon. With that the three nobles collapsed, exhausted.

The eight horses, terrified by the nearness of the desert monster, bolted. They snorted and leapt into running. Having at last received their horrible cargo, they outraced the wind. They sped over the limestone hills, overleaping ravines and flying by boulders.

Some villagers saw the far dust of the huge cart and rang the bell for gathering. Everyone ran to the desert's edge, anxious to see the captive in the cart. When the horses reached the edge of the desert, the villagers waved them to a halt. They knew from the terror in the horses' eyes that the devil indeed had been grappled with and caught.

But when, with great caution, the bravest of them looked over the high walls of the wagon, they saw only the exhausted, much battered, nobles three.

Theme and Resonating Scripture
Source of Evil
Samuel 12, 1-7

NO MAGIC IN THE CAMERA

This is the story of a man of many cameras.
But this story tells of the time when his many
cameras were gone. He had come, so it
happened, on hard days. He no longer had
money enough for film. Indeed, to pay for
food and shelter, he had sold all of his
picture-makers. He had sold all but one.

This is the story of the selling finally of the
last of many cameras. The pain of this sale—
as of this tale—comes because this last camera
was the man's most precious. It was the one
he saved for special days when the light
had an edge of mystery or when pictures of
love were needed. This was the one camera
that bore a name; Fortunato, he called it, as his
father long ago had called him.

He did not want to sell it, had sworn he
never would. It was the picture-maker of all
his joy. What special things he knew of the
world, of living, of himself had leapt at him
with light through the tiny hole that held the
film. It was this camera of fortune that caught
images of light and hope that others lost in
shadow. He had sworn indeed never to sell.
But at the time of oath his belly was full. By the
time of this story it was even less than empty.
It was sell the camera, last and best, or die.
And oh, he thought as he left his room for
the marketplace, it may yet be both: to sell and

then to die.

He had not gone very far with his camera of fortune when, though he was quite hungry, he wished not for food but for one last roll of film. One last hour of seeing, sighting, and snapping the seizure. But it was just a wish. He had no film.

Which is why what he did then was very strange. He saw a boy on the climb of a high link fence. It may have been the boy's eyes or the way the sun made haze behind him or the strain of his fingers in holding tight. There was something that made Fortunato lift the empty camera to his eye, focus quickly on the face in the fence and, without thinking, push the shutter button down. Click.

With that much suddenness the world stopped. Fortunato found himself all at once within the frame. He himself on the fence, straining, lifting at the side of the young boy. There was no sound, no movement, no wind even. Fortunato looked at his young companion, saw him frozen in his effort, saw the harsh pain of high fence climbing, of struggling to overgo the iron links of time. Fortunato's fingers were twisted, cut by his own weight, and the desperation to be on top and over and down again pressed him and made him heavier than ever. When he looked down at the ground and thought of falling, he knew terror and he knew what he had seen in the young boy's eyes, and he knew, quite simply, the young boy. He knew him as he had never known another. Click.

The shutter-button released itself and Fortunato was picture-taker again, distant but different. He was not sure what had happened, but the boy was climbing still and still known. "It may be," he thought, "that this picture-maker, when used without film, makes film of my mind, for that moment is there still living, past but present. I will be a young, desperate, iron-link climber forever."

Fortunato continued on his way toward the marketplace. He thought of the money-man, how hard he was. How very much a pawnbroker. All the other cameras were his now, and soon would be the last, the best. Fortunato wondered then about what had just happened with this last camera—the mystery shift to fence-climbing, the making of his mind to film. He wondered if the money-man would be less hard for such a camera.

At that moment Fortunato was seized anew, now by, of all things, a single, simple, blade of grass. He sighted and focused and snapped, click, and was at once himself tall, thin, slightly green, only inches high, bowed by heavy pellets of mist. The softest breeze wafted him and he made this discovery—that low-down earth-bound wind is kind and warm. Then click, he was back again and the world resumed itself.

Immediately this man of fortune's camera focused again. He was beginning to feel that the small black box between his hands had become an energy of its own. He was within the strong caress of gentle worlds, and the camera he carried made it so. Click, the shutter down, and he was one of several candy-eaters five years old. The taffy-world held itself still, if sticky. It was the moment of delightful tortured teeth, of jaw pulling for no purpose but sweetness. Click.

And click again. He was a hunchbacked passer-by. For a frozen moment in which only he of all the world was watching, he was withered of bone and tired of passing-by. He discovered that, surprisingly, there is no back pain to being a hunched over man, no pain of flesh at all. But there is a pain about being that is everything. It is what happens when, having shuffled home alone, one regrets his arrival at the door. Click.

Fortunato lowered the camera from his face. He saw the quiver of his hands. He knew the quiver of his heart without seeing. It was as if the camera were a pulser of his blood, making it quicker to rush up in blushing or out in bleeding. What seemed an ordinary picture-maker was an entrance way to worlds of other whispers. What seemed a camera without film was in fact a piece of magic, a portable enchanter that made time hold its breath long enough for fortune to be stunned.

Oh, how he would hate to lose it now! A life was given him in this last and best camera. But the death of old hunger was ever in the near shadow. Fortunato needed bread more than he needed the wonder of worlds fully alive for him.

And so it was that this man who had once owned many cameras came to the marketplace with his last and truly best. So it was that Fortunato entered the shop of the money-man desperate enough to bargain with his always loved if newly known last camera.

"Hello," Fortunato said. The pawnbroker said nothing. He looked out from the cage of his counter. Fortunato held up the camera and said, "I've come with my last one."

"I'll give you seven," said the money-man.

"No, wait," Fortunato said. "This one is different. This is no ordinary picture-maker. This camera has a magic in it."

The money-man repeated with the very same voice "I'll give you seven." One of the lenses of his eyeglasses was cracked.

Fortunato said, "You don't understand. One uses no film with this camera. One's mind and heart are film enough. This camera has magic in it."

The pawnbroker said, "I'll give you five." Fortunato could see that something was stirring in the money-man—anger, impatience to be alone, perhaps. He did not believe. His fist was closed and hard on the counter. His eyes were like the dull surface of water on days without sun.

Then without warning Fortunato lifted the box to his face. He saw the cracked lens, sighted, focused, and though the money-man pulled back, he pressed the button for shutter release. Then, click, came the crack of a left eye's lens. All the world was broken in two; there was a jagged wound through the heart of everything. The man of fortune's camera saw the world as the money-man did, cracked and caged and terrified. There was a dusty memory in a frame on the wall—a lady and children, taffy eaters surely. It was clear how loved once they were and how, by now, they were all gone. The money-man, Fortunato saw in that quick, held-breath shot, was empty but for money and the broken dreams of other men. He would buy and hold the cracked hearts of hunger, having despaired of ever finding wholeness or hope in men.

And then the click of the breath release and Fortunato was himself again. He lowered the camera from his face, though his eyes held the focus of before. He saw the money-man seeing him and neither spoke. Fortunato felt the crack of the man, and his own heart was breaking. He wanted only to reach through the cage of the counter and caress the gnarled life of the hard money-man.

And, strange, it was as if the pawnbroker knew all this. He held fast to Fortunato's eyes. Without speaking he lifted his hand and slowly removed his eyeglasses and with them the cracked left lens. In that swift moment, it was as if the crack through the heart of the world was healed. Fortunato and the money-man mingled eyes. The pawnbroker, not soft certainly, was not hard in the way of before. His fist was gone. Without speaking he put out his hand. Fortunato returned the silence and gave with gentleness away the camera, his last and best. The money-man held the camera and, with the way of one who knew such things, examined it and said, "There is no magic in the camera."

Fortunato thought for a moment, remembering the wonder of moments before. He said then, "But sir, we—you and I—are newly met. We are together." "Yes, we are," the money-man said. "But the magic, you see, is You."

Fortunato, seeing on the counter the cracked left lens again, said, "Ah, sir, yes, and You."

Theme and Resonating Scripture
Blind Men See
John 9, 1-7. 35-38

THE TUMBLER AND THE PRINCESS

Once, when life was simpler and men were too, there lived a tumbler who was by far the most skilled and agile acrobat in all the realm. Why, he had even been summoned to court once to perform before the king. All the people, including his highness, were awed by the great daring, the great strength, the great swiftness of his tricks. He was indeed an excellent tumbler and, by and by, the entire realm admired him and regarded him very well. Which was a pleasant turn for the tumbler at first, but, as it turned out, a very bad one.

It so happened, you see, that there was an ill-tempered seer in the realm. He did not like anyone, but he liked least of all those people for whom the kingdom as a whole had high regard. It may be that the ill-tempered seer felt this way because he himself was so little honored. He had in fact been disgraced since his youth when, as the royal seer, he had displeased the king with some of what he saw. He had been abruptly dismissed from the court and had been seeking revenge ever since, revenge against the king and against anyone the king honored.

So it was that when the tumbler was acclaimed by the people and received with graciousness by the king, the ill-tempered seer took notice. He decided to pay a night visit to the acrobat. Now the seer was not a violent sort of man. He would take no pleasure in hitting someone, but he took great pleasure in **seeing**—for he was indeed a seer. So it was that, late one night when the acrobat was sleeping, the ill-tempered seer looked through the window of the acrobat's house and through the window of his sleeping eyes. The seer took great delight in what he saw, wanting as he did the vengeance of a lifetime. The seer, in looking hard at the tumbler, saw clear through to his heart. And he saw that his heart was seriously cracked. There were clear, deep faults running through the middle of his inmost beating self. The tumbler's heart was as fragile as china-lace. It was nearly about to break.

The ill-tempered seer left a message for the tumbler. The message said, simply: "O acrobat of excellence, beware. You are the bearer of a deep-cracked heart. A deep-cracked heart is dangerous and serious for any man, but for one whose life is tumbling, such as yours, a deep-cracked heart is dangerous and deadly."

The tumbler was surprised that morning to find the message, and he was stunned to read it. If his heart was cracked, his very life was. Indeed, if his heart was fragile, his life as a daring tumbler was broken. An acrobat needs many things, but most of all a heart of granite strength that will not break with much hard use.

"It cannot be so," he said. But the seer saw only what was true, and the tumbler knew the cold shaft of real sight immediately. On reading the message the first time, he knew the fast wash of truth. His heart was cracked indeed. For the first time ever he felt it so and his spirit groaned.

From that day on the tumbler could not bring himself to tumble any more. It was not that he'd lost his daring courage exactly. But what man wants a broken heart? If his heart was deeply-cracked already, caution would come as a reflex. So it was with the tumbler. Even if he chose otherwise, his body simply would not curl and hurl itself any longer. Even in plain walking he was slower, more certain of foot, more wary of tripstones. When, not long after this, the tumbler was summoned again to perform for the king, he refused. The king, of course, was angry, for he was celebrating the coming-of-age of his beautiful daughter. All the people of the realm began to say that the tumbler who would not tumble had lost his nerve. He was jeered at wherever he went. Even children, once his greatest admirers, derided him. In this way he was disgraced and the ill-tempered seer had his vengeance.

The tumbler decided to leave the realm, so dishonored had he come to be. The road to the outlands of the kingdom and beyond happened to pass the castle, and it happened also that the day on which the tumbler set out was the day of the king's daughter's coming-of-age. So it was that as the tumbler drew near to the castle he saw a great crowd gathered. All the people of the realm had come to honor the king's beautiful daughter.

But there was something wrong. When the tumbler joined the far edges of the people he heard the low murmur of gathered fear.

"What is wrong?" the tumbler asked a farmer.

"The lovely young princess there," was the reply. The tumbler looked to where the farmer pointed. He saw the king's beautiful daughter dearly clutching a narrow ledge on the castle's high south tower.

"How came she there?" the tumbler asked. Several standers-by then told him of the morning's strange events. Everyone had been gathered in the large center yard and the king was about to present his daughter with the robe of her majority. It was a happy moment, for all the realm dearly loved the beautiful girl. But the moment of her honor had been harshly interrupted. The one known as the ill-tempered seer broke upon the circle of lords and ladies and, in front of the whole assembled realm, he had furiously vilified her. When the tumbler asked of the standers-by what the seer had said of the princess, they hesitated until one of them said in quick whispers, "He said she was not perfect nor beautiful as she seemed. He said her very heart was cracked. And the princess, very, very disturbed by this, ran weeping from the yard. She ran to the tower and found that ledge." When this was said everyone drew back, as if they didn't want to hear it again.

But the tumbler dropped his traveling bundle and pushed his way through the crowd to the tower of the castle. When he reached the wall, he stopped and looked up its steep face. He felt the familiar fear, but only briefly. Then he was climbing, sure as shadows and quick as any bird. With all his old agility he made his way from foothold to handhold, from occasional gaps in the stone to small protrusions. A new and total stillness fell over the crowd as it saw the once-favored tumbler on the climb.

When he neared the ledge he called up to the king's daughter, "Highness, hold fast." And then he was there, clinging hard himself to the narrow ridge of her holding.

The tumbler looked at the princess. She was weeping still. Her eyes were fast closed. She was indeed quite beautiful, but her fear was catching. The tumbler looked down at the ground himself, and what he saw then nearly caused him to lose his hold on the narrow ridge. What he saw then was a massive crowd of worried, fearful, craning men, each one of whom bore a deep-cracked heart. What the seer had said of the tumbler and the princess was true, but so was it true of everyone. The tumbler gestured down to the crowd for the princess to see. She looked and saw and slowly smiled her tears away.

The tumbler said to the princess, "Highness, hold me." He offered his hand and she took it. She held to him fast. Slowly they began to make their way down the steep face of the castle tower wall. They almost made it safely to the ground, but, when they were still high enough to hurt, the tumbler, tired by then, lost his hold and fell. He and the princess crashed to the ground.

They did not die, but, indeed, fell into laughter where they lay. They still held each other, but it was, as the crowd could see, less clinging than embrace. All the people smiled to see them well and laughing so. But, at that moment, the ill-tempered seer stepped forward from the crowd. Everyone fell back, for everyone was afraid the seer would look at him and see too well. The seer was quite disturbed, not only that the princess would yet be honored, but that the tumbler would

surely yet be honored again. So it was that
the ill-tempered seer, with all the fury he
could muster, said, "Stop laughing so! Stop
laughing or your deep-cracked hearts will
break."

The princess and the tumbler, still holding
each other, let their laughter rest. The tumbler
looked at the seer and said, "Sir, our
deep-cracked hearts have broken already.
We have broken them on this falling. We have
broken them on this sharing of laughter."

"Why laughter?" the seer asked.

"Because," the tumbler said, "the crack in
the heart breaks not for nothing but for giving
away."

The princess, like a true princess then said:
"The breaking of a heart is the breaking at
last of love." She said it gently, without
reproach, for the newly-fallen princess was
seeing the sad seer, and a piece of her heart
went to him.

Theme and Resonating Scripture
Unexpected Grace
Judith 16, 1-7

Eucharistic Prayer

EUCHARISTIC PRAYER

       . . . after a tale, out of wonder

Brothers and sisters, let us open our ears
  to the old story.
Let us make it new again.
It is the story about this bread, this wine,
  which come of the hard labor of poor men,
  which come of the hard labor of rain and
  earth, and air and fire and time,
  which gather into themselves now
all the yearnings of each of us.
As we hand over these symbols of our care
  to our Father in Jesus,
  we hand over ourselves to each other.
Let us declare the stillness out of which
  the awesome Word of God might leap.
  Let us be quiet and pray.
       (Silence for some moments)

Spirit of God, Spirit of Jesus,
  breathe among us now.
Come from the four winds
  to open our ears
  so that we can hear your Word of power,
  to ready our hearts
  so that we can feel your Word of tenderness.
Breathe life into our many kinds of death
  and make of these offerings,
  born of our shared yearnings,
  the body and the blood of our Lord Jesus.

Father, it was not yesterday
   that your care for us began,
   but it was, as you say, in the beginning.
In the beginning you spoke
   and the world was made
   and the story started
   and the tale told.
It was the tale of your great love.
In the hearts of history's children,
   the first men, our first fathers and mothers,
   you planted your Word.
And they spun it out, spoke it,
   haltingly, obscurely, but true.
You chose among them Abraham
   and the battered line of his sons and
      daughters.
   They were to be the great tellers of your
      tale.
   Like us they were men of poor memory
   and again and again they forgot.
You sent them prophets and poets
   burdened with your vision,
   burning with your dream,
   always saying this is so;
   the yearnings of our hearts are messages
      from you.
But there were other tales to tell,
   other words to hear.
   Our fathers were not faithful.

And so it was you did the deed,

the completely unexpected one.
You took the timeless hopes of men,
    the search since once-upon-a-time
    for light and one true Word of love.
You took the ancient yearnings of men
    and you made of them a man.

He had been your very own from all ever,
    your Word of love himself.
He took the flesh of Nazareth,
    our sister Mary's very own.
He grew to tell the tale of your love,
    shouted out the coming of your kingdom.
But we were busy with other words again
    and so it was that we took the man
    who was our own best hope
    and one day in time
    we killed him.
We nailed him to a pole.
Yet here we are gathered round him.
    We witness, celebrate, proclaim
    the transforming by you
    of his death into life,
    of our sin into salvation,
    of this bread and wine
    into his flesh and blood—
    for the life of the world.

For, on the night on which he was handed
        over,
    the night before he died,

Jesus took bread, broke it
and gave it to his friends, saying,
"Take this and eat it, all of you.
This is my body. It will be broken for you."
And then he took the cup and he said
"Take this cup and drink from it.
It is the cup of my blood,
the blood that makes binding
the new promise you have in me forever.
It is the cup
that will be poured out
so that your sins will be forgiven.
Remember me by doing this."

We delight to remember him by doing this,
    Lord God.
  We tell the tale again
  of your great gifts to us,
  beginning with the beginning,
  coming to now,
  ending only with the end
  when the last and best catastrophe
  will sweep over us,
  a gentle flood of your care,
  the final coming of Jesus again.

Remembering him, Lord God, we thank you.
  By his presence under these signs,
  bread, wine, ourselves,
  we thank you, Father.

Remembering him, Lord God, we recommit
     ourselves
   to you and to each other.
   We dare to accept again
   your foolish choice of us
   as tellers of your tale.

Give us new hearts, new tongues,
   hearts and tongues of the Spirit,
   new awareness of the intensity of life
   around us and within us,
   so that we might tell it well and truly,
   so that we might be images of hope to the
     despairing,
   givers of your good news
   to this nearly hardened world of ours,
   this world you embrace in Jesus Christ,
     our Lord,
   this world in whose most hidden fantasy
   you take great delight in Jesus Christ,
     our Lord
Through whom you give us
   laughter
   and fairy tales
   and all other signs of life.
Through whom we give you
   thanks
   and praise
   now and evermore. Amen.